Teaching!

"Your Failure To Improve Your Own Teaching Is _Greater_ Than The Students' Disinterest"

10 Effective Practices For Teachers Of God's Word!

Abb Thomas

Abb Thomas 5978 Katey Way, Milford, Ohio, 45150 (513) 313-5610
TrainingTeachers.org

ISBN 0-9779399-2-8

Printed in the United States of America by John the Baptist Publishing, Milford, Ohio.

Dedication

After forty years of personal study and experience alongside large groups of wonderful teachers, the needs seen have been great. The books I have read from my predecessors have taught me what I had never learned before. The great passion I have read (between the lines) has moved me and stirred my own heart to go farther, to add to, and to become better for my Lord. Clarity is a must. Focus in study, wisdom, knowledge and understanding that comes from God are all essential for the teacher of God's Word.

This work is based on all these years of travel, listening, reading, and trying to experience what is needed both in preparation and presentation of a lesson. It is filled with what I believe thousands of teachers for God have never heard. May it be that kind of help!

So, I dedicate this work to the church of our living God, and to those that teach the Word of God week after week. May you improve greatly!

Abb Thomas

Teaching

*"Your Failure to Improve Your Own Teaching
Is <u>Greater</u> Than The Students Disinterest"*

Introduction: In this study we are touching some of the crucial areas that must bring a clear understanding to teachers of their role. We will think through the process that could reward you with real learning taking place within your classroom week after week. There are ways to verify learning, if we are willing to see the results. There are processes that will assure us that learning could take place in our class each week. We cannot make students learn. You cannot swat them with your big black Bible and say, "Learn, learn. What's wrong with you?" I know you have thought about that before, perhaps even bringing a ball bat to class.

In our classroom, they could learn if they would learn. That is our goal. We want to be sure that those steps are in place each week. Perhaps we can learn a few things that still need to be in place from our side of the classroom. Some things suggested, you will say, "Oh, I've known that for years." Yes, but how long has it been since you taught that way? Keep an open mind as you proceed. Take notes, underline, stop now and then and brainstorm yourself with the last two paragraphs you just read. Creativity comes from *reading and thinking*. I will give you some thoughts to read, then, you stop along the way and think it through.

Please understand, no author on teaching has yet to arrive him/herself.

"When you're through improving, you're through," someone said. I just turned seventy in age, just completed forty years of ministry in two large churches, have read every book I can find on teaching and ministry, and yet I feel so inadequate to even record my own thoughts. Until I can no longer read or hear a book read I will read them all. If there is a better way to say it, better way to illustrate it, that is what I want. You can have my old illustration, because I now have a better one.

Of course the highest motivation is not just to improve myself, but to make myself better for the sake of Christ and the communication of His Word! I know you feel the same. So, let us read again some ideas, think them through, remind our self of the great significance of our role as teacher, and rededicate our self to this role.

Contents
10 Effective Qualities For Teachers!

Introduction

Conclusion

Chapter ONE
Teacher Characteristics

Suggestions for this section:

Yes, I have listed **fifty** of what I would call styles or characteristics of good teachers. There are more, but this is enough for most of us.

You may choose:

1) Read through them all at one time. However, guard against comparing every characteristic with your present style, then looking for the resignation form to turn in. *Let this list give you goals for the next two years!*

We all fall short of perfection, but the goal is to keep striving that we become better and better for our Lord!

2) Or, choose to read the first ten, and then go to chapter two. Read eleven through twenty, then read chapter three as you work your way through the book.

In multiple spots throughout the book, read a concept, then take time to "think it through" in light of your experience, preparation time, facilities, classroom time, and the present response level of your students. No one teaches your class but you.

Learn as you go, on the spot, which will help the ideas to "fit" you and your students. Take your time. Let the notes saturate your thoughts as you go. This is not a book to speed-read in order to get it on your shelf as soon as possible. If this book need not be ever read again, perhaps there was not much worthy of reading the first time.

Underline key thoughts, quotes, and one-liners. These thoughts will be the ones that hold the most value as you review them often enough that it becomes the way you teach!

Teacher Characteristics

1. They teach one "big idea" or "main point," not multiple points.
Teachers know that people do not make multiple decisions per session anyway. If I can get one point across clearly and thoroughly, I have done about all I can do. Too many ideas actually break up the full impact of the first point you made. Sometimes, too much is just too much.

2. They do not teach more, they teach less (content) with more focus.
When we teach less, it means we now have more time to illustrate the one truth two, three, or four times to make sure everyone understands. More content means that less will be covered thoroughly. More content means that less learning styles of students will be touched during the lesson. The total

content reduces the use of visuals, stories, illustrations, and other techniques. There is not time left to use them.

3. They involve the God-given senses.

The senses go all around the world, cross all cultural boundaries, and help to insure us the ability to learn best as soon as possible. Students learn best and retain best when the senses are engaged. God gave senses for us to learn by.

4. They cause thinking to take place in their classroom.

It is the teacher's responsibility to cause thinking to take place. If the student has not been thinking his way through the lesson, he is not ready to arrive at a decision at the end of the lesson. He may arrive at your decision, but that may not change his life at all. In your lesson preparation, what questions will cause thinking?

5. They slow down in talk to match the understanding level of their students.

It is not that some teachers talk too fast (speed of talk), but that many of us just keep on talking as if the student understands about as much as we do. You must pause along the way to see if the student is still with you. You will never know if you never ask.

6. They "master" teaching techniques that help clarify God's truth.

There are literally hundreds of techniques for teachers to use. Some you will use repeatedly for years to come. When you study methods and practice methods, you will always be ready to adapt or adjust to any classroom of students. Techniques assist the teacher to help students to learn above the method of talk alone.

7. They understand that if they do not have the students' attention, something else still does. You can begin by talking to students or to the wall. All ages of students have far more to think about than what you are planning to say. Teens have boys or girls on their mind, cell phones, dates, sports, etc. Adults have last week's problems on their mind, as well as next week's problems, teenagers, credit cards, etc. Children have play things in their pockets, or who is making the funniest faces on their minds.

8. They know that silence and strict discipline often cause a lack of learning.

When all the effort is to keep everyone silent, there is not time for active learning to take place. Without classroom involvement, the student may also not be involved with their mind. Your talking for the next thirty-five minutes may not be what a child or even an adult needs at all.

9. They know without question that learning is active, not passive.

There is not a book in the world that tells the learner to sit there, do nothing, see nothing, say nothing, write nothing, go home with nothing, and you will retain it all. It is the exact opposite. When the class is designed to just sit and listen, almost every principle of learning is ignored. Lecture is part, but only a part.

10. They clearly identify the application in real life.

Application saturates the lesson for a teacher who anticipates life change at the end of the lesson. Application cannot be a one liner, "We all ought to live like that," at the last minute of class. Why did you teach that lesson anyway? Application means applied to life. That is the higher level of teaching. You will prepare more, pray more, and anticipate change more when you believe that God can change the lives of your students right in your classroom!

11. "Never let the lunatics run the asylum." Winston Churchill
You can have much classroom involvement, which helps learning in a great way, and yet not allow the students to go "bananas." Involvement maximizes learning in the hearts of any age group. It is how we learn best and retain best. Getting students involved causes learning which causes interest in your students.

12. Adult teachers realize that older saints have significant comments to lend to the lesson. Never forget that older folks have good comments to add, they just never have an opportunity in most classes. They have already heard ten thousand messages and seven thousand lessons. Some have walked with God for the last thirty, forty, or fifty years; and have good thought from bad and good experiences of life. Most just have no place to express it because the teacher does not allow time for discussion.

13. Good teachers "think through" the best choices of words and terms to use with their students. As you prepare your lesson, look for the words and terms that will need a definition or an illustration. That becomes part of your lesson plan. As a teacher you realize that you know what you are saying, but you are not talking to you. You are talking to whoever sits in front of you and at their level of understanding. Your role is to so clarify what God has to say that the student cannot possibly miss it. That is who you are and what you do!

14. Teachers practice their emotions and mannerisms in order to add life and meaning to the words used. Remember that 93% of communication comes from above the words you say. Therefore the good teacher will often practice their lesson in front of a mirror to watch their own expressions, or the lack thereof. Teachers read the Bible passage aloud in order to hear their own voice and how they are saying what they read. Teachers have never sat in the audience and watched themselves teach. If they did, there would be changes made immediately.

15. Visuals are a main-stay to teaching, regardless of the age of students.
Yes, it often takes that extra effort to have visuals ready for class, but the great value of helping your students to retain what you taught is worth it all. Students retain at least 50% of what they see. It is often the most remembered part of the lesson. Whether it be a flat picture shown, a handmade poster board, a white board, an overhead projector, or a story vividly told, the visual pictured in one's mind will stay there for a long time. It is worth your effort!

16. They allow the Spirit of God to be in on their preparation and their presentation time. Every teacher has heard that the Holy Spirit of God is the teacher of all teachers. He is our teacher. The big question is: do we allow Him to do what He can do in us as we prepare to teach the Word of God? He is there and willing to impress us with the most significant thoughts and verses and goals for our lesson. We must start early in the week to give Him time to teach us. It sure is a lonely road to take when we do not allow Him to squeeze into our time of lesson preparation.

17. They begin lesson preparation early enough to be able to "master" the lesson.
We will spend a chapter ahead on mastering your lesson. The teacher learns to select less total content, but the best of all they have in order to be able to master their lesson. Instead of the normal eight to nine pages of notes, they now come to class with less total stuff, which means they have more time to get less content across thoroughly. The better teacher comes to class with

one page or less of notes, with only a small reminder note of what comes next in the lesson order.

18. They are willing to take a risk to try out a new method or technique. The person you would call "creative" is the one who always has ideas going in his classroom that cause students not only to enjoy the class, but to listen well enough to understand the point of it all, and to retain it longer. There is a reason for that, and it is because that teacher is always looking for those methods and techniques that will help him teach. They realize that using a new idea that does not work well is not a reflection on them. It is a reflection on it (the idea). So it is very simple. Try another one, and success comes! The creative person is creative because he reads, thinks it through, and tries another idea.

19. The attitude of the teacher sets the tone of the student response within the class. The teacher only has to think back to his own classroom days when he was the student. What made the difference between one teacher and another? Most, we would admit was the way they presented themselves. You enjoyed the class or you hated to go. You sat down in one class with anticipation of an enjoyable class and for learning to take place. Another class you anticipated the worst, and so it always seemed to be that way. The teacher is responsible for setting the mood, the atmosphere, and the anticipation for class. It often begins when the teacher takes stock of how he thinks of the students, thus those thoughts influence how he approaches the class time. Sometimes, both sides seem to be on the defense.

20. They know they cannot "make" people learn, but in their classroom they could learn if they would learn. Therefore, the aggressive teacher is going out of his way to learn all the principles we list here and to use them often. Students are used to just "sitting and listening" for several years. Our classes have often taught them to sit motionless and speechless and wait until it is over, like the last time and the time before that. Even though the principle says that learning is active, not passive, we can agree with it and yet teach the exact opposite. It has been done for years, and probably in our church.

21. They know that the accumulation of content is not the goal – life-change is the goal! If your goal is that the students will know more about the Bible this week than last week, after your lesson, then just say your little prayer and go home. Yes, growing in knowledge of the Bible is a goal, but it is a life-long goal. However, the immediate goal and the greater goal is that the truth will change someone's life, even in our classroom! Why can the Word change a person's life at the church altar, but we have not seen that happen in our classroom in years? Why is that? I believe it is because we never allow time for it to happen. But, it can!

22. They know that the learning process is not to be ignored.

There is always a process that takes us from where we start to where we need to go. The process used in this book is simple, but covers the basis that could insure that learning could take place if the student would allow it. The same process can help to organize your lesson. I meet teachers all across this country who have taught for thirty years and never one time have ever even heard of a process that could insure learning. They have assumed for years that their dry as dust lecture has somehow, in some way, been of help. Let us not forget that the Word of God is not void of people's interest. Perhaps we have never verified learning within our students.

23. To the best of their ability, teachers get to know their students.

Not just by name, but by need is the best way to know who you teach. Unless I know something about the everyday life and dreams and goals of my students, how can I pray well for them? My prayers must be very "general," such as "Lord, bless my class next week." Too general, nothing specific, just "bless'em all." Sorry, that is not good enough. The more you know of who you teach, the better teacher you become. Now you go home and prepare your lesson in light of who you teach. That is a better way!

24. They know that content is the <u>what</u>, application is the <u>so what</u>.
Content represents everything that is said throughout your class time. Application is like, "So what does all that mean?" If it does not make sense in real life, there is no reason to apply it to life. Since God's Word is from Him, to us, for the purpose of our obedience and our living, then why would the teacher not tell me how it works in real life? Excellent teachers teach 50% content, 50% application. It is not the common way we are used to, but it is the best way.

25. A good teacher does not assume that church people already know words and terms well. As you prepare your lesson, assume that most students do not have a good understanding of the truth you plan to teach. There are some good things to assume. Assume that with most key words or terms you will use, some of your students will not understand without a very clear definition and perhaps an illustration. Assume that most of your students need this truth in their lives today. Assume that some students will never hear you teach again. Assume that some students do not have a clue as to what this truth really means.

26. Great teachers know that everyone does not have to get saved in five minutes or less. Bringing students to Christ is a very serious matter, never to be taken lightly or in a rushed condition. Caring for such matters hurriedly may find us back to assuming the student understood thoroughly enough for genuine belief to take place. What about the Spirit of God and His part in the matter? What about understanding? What about the seed, the soil, and the other spiritual conditions of such great decisions? A clear understanding simply helps us to do a good job in explanation considering this great truth!

27. Teachers know that the difference between the ordinary and the extra - ordinary is the extra! When you come into a classroom where the whole hour is different than you have experienced before, it is because the teacher is that different part. He has put more time and effort than the ordinary teacher has into the lesson preparation. He has probably prayed more too. Everything is not to make him look good, but to make the truth look very inviting. That is why there is classroom involvement, visuals, time to discuss a matter, more than one illustration, and everyone in the class has had the truth thoroughly explained. The teacher has so clarified the truth that the whole class could not possibly miss it.

28. Great teachers know that the lesson is only as good as they (the students) understand it. Talk for two hours if you wish, but if they do not "get it," nothing is going to happen. Therefore, in your preparation week, work hard with the students' understanding in mind. Add another illustration, another role play, and be careful to explain all the tough words and terms. In other words, do not show up unless you are prepared to really teach.

29. They know that covering all the material is not the goal.
The teacher must learn early that all the material in front of you (such as a quarterly) is not equal in value for the student. The real goal is to choose less total content, such as 40-50-60%, and forget about the rest. The amount

of content is not as significant as the choice of content. Does it touch your students where they are living? Sometimes, the spirit of the class may dictate that we drop part of the lesson because a discussion or comment led to a much more important session than we actually had planned. Allow God to take over your class at any time!

30. They know that students do not learn multiple lessons in a single session.

When the teacher comes to class with 4-5-6 points, it is hard enough to keep all six in view, much less to cover each and to tie them all together with the main thought. Sometimes we just give too much. By the time we hit point five, Leroy has already forgotten 1-2-3 and 4. You can better concentrate by focusing in on one main truth and illustrating that same truth four or five ways. Illustrations, all pointing to the same part of life simply help all students to have a better opportunity of seeing the one main truth within their circumstances, as compared to different circumstances in the lives of others. The main thrust is still there, allowing all students to see it in real life, their real life!

31. They know that their lesson needs a definite direction.

Why are you teaching this lesson anyway? Where are you heading? Where do you want your students to go with this truth? How will they get there? It is the purpose of your lesson before you begin your lesson. If the student could actually hear me teach, then walk out the classroom door and still not know HOW to live like that in real life, I don't believe I have taught. Almost every lesson you will teach is for living. It is for our obedience to God's Word. A lesson without direction does not go anywhere. Of course, we all know that. I have been in classes where the teacher would have done us a favor if he had just told us up front that there is no real purpose for this lesson. So, what is your destination?

32. Teachers know that at best "more stuff" (content) means that "less" will be covered thoroughly. One of the major problems in our classrooms is that teachers come to class with too much stuff. We have nine pages of notes and we have convinced ourselves that if we have time to say "all of that," surely they will get it. But, that is not how people learn best and not how they retain best. But, we do it anyway. If I can start as soon as possible, talk as fast as I can for as long as I can, "they'll get it." That is a problem. When we have too much stuff, we will forfeit our time to say the main thing twice, or explain critical words that need to be understood. We have no time to use the God-given senses (the way students learn best). We know all of that; but if it does not seem to bother us, it should.

33. Teachers know that all content is not equally important.
As we select the 40-50-or 60% slices out of all the content in front of us, we must learn how to skim all the rest aside without remorse. Normally the content in front of you has a lot of "peripheral" thoughts. They are not bad, but they will only gradually get you to what you have really come to say. Do not take twenty-five minutes to get to what you intend to get across. Then you only have fifteen minutes to say what you really wanted to say all along. Get there within five minutes, and then spend all your time saying what you came to say. Great things will happen in your class!

34. Great teachers bridge the gap between hundreds of years ago and today.
There are plenty of Bible illustrations of Bible times, customs, and lands. Use these, but also use the current items that your students of today use all the time. We have to bring the thoughts to be current with the students' thoughts,

if we intend to keep the attention. It is just that what fills our students' minds today are computers, video games, cell phones, e-mails, texting, etc., which were not in the vocabulary of Bible folks. Current illustrations also include the daily news of the world and especially of your local area. A local event appeals to the mind more than what is ancient to our life today. That is not a bad reflection on Bible times of the past, it is just that the current life styles draw more attention and retain attention better. Therefore, use both!

35. Teachers know that "learning is unpleasant only if it seems useless or irrelevant" (*Making Your Teaching Count* by Willis). One of our major points of teaching is to use the learning process to organize your lesson to assure that learning could take place if the student would allow it. Step three in that process is stated as To Personalize. Here is where the learner must identify himself in the truth you give. It is when "I see me in this truth." The lesson is not just about Abraham or Moses, Peter, Paul, James, or John; but "I see me in this truth"! It must strike home. It must come to this "good 'ol boy," which is me. When the lesson is not personalized, then the student sees little necessity to keep listening. It is about someone else. That is why the teacher cannot skip or weaken this part of the lesson.

36. Great teachers know that teaching without application is fruitless.
Content alone does not change lives. Content must be wedded with application if results have a possibility of happening. How many hundreds of lessons have I heard in these sixty plus years that have been jam-packed with content (notes and notes and notes), then when the last minute of class arrives it is always the same: "You know kids, teens, or adults, we all "ought to live like that." Well let us pray, "God help us to live like that, Amen." We now all walk out the classroom door, having heard for the "umpteenth" time that we "ought to," but most still do not have a clue "how to" live like that in

real life, at home, at school, at the work place. No time was left to commit that area of life to the Lord.

37. The teacher's role is not to blame the student for his distant looks, but to counteract boredom, disinterest, and distractions. Wow, that sounds like it is all my fault. No, the student has a lot of mischief built in from his home training, peer friends, etc.; but I need to assume the role of providing a classroom where there is no time for minds to wander. I am not talking of speaking so many words that they have no time for that. That may be a major part of the problem right there. As teacher, I must take on the challenge to read as much as possible in books that would help me to counter act discipline problems. Books are written that are filled with great ideas. The authors have been exactly where you are and have come up with some answers.

38. They know that boring teachers counter act the force of persuasion. I do not have to describe what it is like to sit through a boring class. We have all been there. We dread even walking into the room. The mind is spent reminding you how boring this is and to keep watching your clock (the only hope you have). You just missed a marvelous statement or verse that could have solved a nagging problem for you, but your mind was on the suffering you were going through. In order to not be that kind of teacher, you then declare that you will educate yourself to be that extraordinary teacher!

39. They know that a better presentation will probably require a better preparation. Whatever is better than before will undoubtedly take more time and effort. To be the teacher with the outstanding presentation, that teacher must do whatever that role requires. Perhaps it is an initial three hour addition in my preparation time. Oh, but that is tough in our busy life styles of today. Whatever you wish to improve, it will take more than what you presently give. But, keep your eyes fixed on the goal, the better goal, the higher level goal! You will be a part of the few who have so dedicated themselves to such a worthy cause. The communication of the Word of God requires and demands the teacher to be at his best always.

40. Because people do not listen well, you must have time to say it again and again.

We have touched on this before, but it demands our attention often. When you determine that key one main point you are walking into class to say, then of all things, you want to say that thought multiple times. Once at the beginning, once in the middle, and once before your final prayer is not enough. If that is your main point, it should be handled as if it is your only point. If they remembered little else when they got home and again tomorrow, what would that one-liner be? That is exactly what should be announced multiple times, up to fifteen times per class. Can they say it, see it, write it, practice it, go home with it? Now you are teaching!

41. Teachers know that more to remember equals less remembered.

The more points or key thoughts or verses used within the class period, equals less remembered. The average teacher, it has been said, will say approximately eight thousand to ten thousand words in a given classroom time, if talking is all that happened in that time. You cannot recall eight thousand words. You cannot even remember the sentence before last the guy used. It sounded good at the moment, but the moment has been swallowed up by thirty-five other such moments. No notes were taken; little to no review, and the paragraphs just kept coming. Sorry, but that is what you get.

42. **When teachers use one-point lessons, everything else you add will support, prove, illustrate, repeat, and make it easier to understand and retain.** It makes good sense, and most of us understand that. However, does it change our teaching? When there is less total ground to cover, we can then focus on covering the main point several times to help different students to grasp it. One student sees it best through a real life illustration, while another understands best through a very clear definition. Another needs a scenario that happens in a home or neighborhood setting. A discussion will allow one or two to ask the exact question that will clear it up for them. An object lesson will help some. But, when there is not time enough to approach the same truth from different angles, some may be left confused.

43. **They know that the Spirit of God is ready, able, waiting, and desiring to help them to prepare their lesson.** Without the Spirit of God giving us direction and selection of content, we are only "talking heads." He is called the Teacher of teachers, and for that alone we should highly desire that He be in full control of us during the week of preparation and on the day of presentation. Do not overlook His ministry, and do not neglect Him until you are pulling into the church parking lot on Sunday. He knows what you have to teach; He knows your students. He lives with them, walks with them, and knows where they are spiritually right now. He is God, and He so desires to teach you this lesson this week before you stand in front of them.

44. **Teachers know that their lesson is not about their quarterly or covering all the material; but is about Zach, Teddy, Sue, and Jeanie, or the widow Jones.** Your lesson is for real live people. They have heard content for years; they need to hear the application of that content into real life. Is that what you give them? The Spirit of God will help you do exactly that. The notes of help you have are an aid, a guide, a help, a suggestion, and are good, but

not all are of equal importance. The goal is not to just cover the notes, but to cover Zach, Teddy, and Sue!

45. Teachers know that their God-given gifts are to be developed further. Gifts, even from your wonderful Creator, come to you not necessarily fully developed. If you would practice those gifts, you would be better than you were before! God has given you the gift to teach. However, without your effort to improve, it is like putting the gifts of God on hold. The singer practices to get better at breath control, range, and tune, just as a teacher practices new methods or techniques. The goal is improvement. Read a book, try some new creative methods. Practice in front of a mirror to improve your facial expressions. Read the story aloud to see just how well you pronounce or emphasize strong emotional words. It all helps, it all improves us.

46. Teachers realize that 93% of communication (what actually comes across) is above and beyond the words you say. I went for years not having a clue of this statement. Finally, after finding the largest studies ever done on communication (what actually comes across), it turns your thinking upside down. Even the Word of God can be presented as if it is the most boring book you have read in the last six months. It is certainly not, but the teacher gave that impression just from his mannerisms. If that is what came across, it is hard to over-ride the feelings you received. But, some work done on our mannerisms will keep that from happening in our class!

47. Teachers know that poor teaching methods and techniques quickly become habitual. It is so easy to get into a rut. The rut has taken our presentation to the boring side of teaching. The students know that complaining does not work, it never has. So, they simply learn to tolerate it again next week. They watch their clock move so slowly, text their friends about ballgames, etc., while I teach and just wait until next year when they are promoted. When we evaluate our teaching, it helps us to clear up those areas. When we choose another teacher to critique us, then we can critique them. It opens our eyes to what we have grown accustomed to doing every week. Habitually using poor techniques lures us all to sleep.

48. Teachers know that their role is to SO clarify what God has to say to the student, that the student could not possibly miss what God has to say to him! This is my definition of who a teacher is and what a teacher does. It is amazing that the great God of heaven still uses people like you and like me to be teachers. In fact, we are the only one in that classroom to do that. That reality drives us to get better and better as a teacher. The very role carries heavy-duty responsibilities if we intend to be that teacher. I must "push myself" to improve. That is why I read. That is why I practice. That is why I try something new!

49. Teachers know the ability to use questions well will enlarge their significance with the student. Questions from students are good for me, because they take my concentration off the lesson to the student. After all, we teach people, more than just lessons. Now my focus is exactly on the need. Questions from you help you to see if the student is still with you. Questions from the student help you to see that he is confused or the need for a bit more clarification. Why would I not want to know that? Benefit from questions, your students will too.

50. Teachers realize that every student is only one prayer away from making everything right with God! I heard this statement over forty years ago and have never forgotten the impact. The unsaved child in your class is only one prayer away from receiving Christ! The biggest gossip in the church is only one prayer away from making everything right with God! Whatever the truth you teach next week, the student that needs it is only one prayer away from having it in their life. Whether it needs to be out of their life or in their life, one prayer will do it. Approach your next week of preparation and your hour of presentation with this thought in mind, and you will find yourself teaching with great passion and compassion.

Chapter TWO

They Could Learn, If They Would Learn, In My Classroom!

They could learn, if they would learn, in my classroom! Chapter two will lay out the learning process in a most simple but necessary plan. There are bases to touch if learning is to be possible in your classroom.

We cannot make students believe or live according to the truth you just taught, but by following the "process," they could learn, if they would learn, in my classroom!

The outline includes:

II. They Could Learn, If They Would Learn, In My Classroom

    1. Step 1 Is To Know

    2. Step 2 Is To Understand

    3. Step 3 Is To Personalize

    4. Step 4 Is To Practice

5. The Final And Ultimate Step

6. Out-Achieving Yourself As A Teacher

7. The Blame Game Is Not For A Teacher

II. They Could Learn, If They Would Learn, In My Classroom!

Teach all you want, but if the students are not "getting it" (*the relevancy in real life),* nothing is going to happen. That is scary, but that is our calling!

We understand that with all the passion and compassion we can muster, we still cannot make students learn. They are free to walk out of our classroom and do the exact opposite before they get home.

However, we also know **that it is not our area of responsibility** to try and "make" students fall into line. The Lord works on the inside (*heart matters),* while we work on the "outside" (*understanding, reasoning, compelling).* That does not diminish our heart-felt concern for the Christ-likeness we would like to see in their life.

To assure that students **could** learn if they **would** learn in our classroom, we prepare our lesson in light of *"The Learning Process."*

Perhaps you have seen different processes used to plan and implement your lesson. I like to break it down into four parts, which cover everything I want to touch, plus leading the whole lesson to a decision for life change.

1. Step 1 is To Know

Here is where our Bible Time begins. We are after *three steps* to be in place during this first six to eight minute time period. *(1) The first part of Step 1 is to read the main Bible passage.* Hopefully, if your students can read, and the passage is not extremely long, ask them to read with you. If the passage has several verses you wish to cover now, use other methods that help students to listen and be involved: read responsively – you read, they read, you read, etc. Occasionally, designate a "good reader" to read the passage. If shorter, all read together as you lead.

We do this because of the *God-given senses*, which help every person worldwide to learn best. Instead of just hearing alone, now they are **hearing, seeing,** and **saying.** It looks as though they would get more out of it. They would, if I would just teach that way. It works with all age groups.

(2) The second part of Step 1 is to give a preview of what God is going to teach us. Maybe list two to three questions that this passage will help us with. You may wish to start with a provocative statement that will be answered.

(3) The third part of Step 1 is to give them a reason to listen. Here we add something to grip them with anticipation. Perhaps I use a "what if" situation. "What if this happened to you?"

For example, I begin with this statement in an adult class: Class, you go to your mailbox, and hanging on the side is a folded sheet. It is from someone on your block. In fact, it is your next door neighbor whom you have tried to befriend for the sake of Christ. Your whole family is invited to a "block-party"! The details include: swimming for the kids, a local small rock band for the teens, and an excellent time to enjoy your neighbors. Bring some picnic foods, and BYOB.

We would have to admit, it is a questionable event to attend, but it is next door and I could meet some other neighbors and . . .

"Now here is the question. Will you be there with your family? ***Does God speak on this issue?*** Could you go for "the sake of Christ," or would your testimony demand you stay away? Turn to verse twelve and let's begin!"

In conclusion, **Step 1** is for this purpose: (1) Read the passage together. (2) Give the gist of what we can learn. (3) Give students a reason to listen.

Our diagram of the learning process will develop like this:

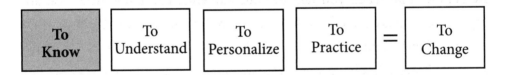

Remember, going into content before they see the need to hear content can very quickly become hard for the student to listen to. There is no real-life **reason** for them to listen. Perhaps I have not been persuasive enough in relating it to real life. What is in it for the person who has to listen to you for the next forty minutes? It is a fair question that the teacher should answer before the students start tuning out.

All ages need a strong reason to listen to help take their attention off a world of other things already on their mind.

Step 1 helps them to know the facts. What does the Bible say? However, head knowledge does not mean that learning has taken place, we are still at Step 1.

Step 2 leads us to help our students To Understand.

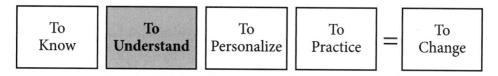

To see what the Bible truth clearly means. So, here we define words and terms, we illustrate, discuss, and allow for questions as needed. Whatever it takes to grasp the truth is our goal. Students who do not discern hard words or new terms will need you to help them. This part of the lesson is that time. Remember that when you talk to your students, you know what you are saying; but you are not talking to yourself, but to the student. And it is at the student's level of understanding, which may be far below yours. You have studied all week, but he has not. You are an ardent student of the Word, but the student probably is not. If you teach a child, then compare your time-developed vocabulary with that of a third grader. Be careful with the words you "assume" that students have learned.

You cannot skip over this step in the process. You cannot assume that your students know this. As you prepare your lesson, you scan the passages for words and terms that some may not understand. It is a must for all ages, including adults.

In many classes, because this time is so shallow, often the student is left behind. They still do not understand what you said four paragraphs ago.

That is the great value of using questions with your students. Surely you would want to know if three or four of your students did not "get" the last five minutes of your lesson. You will never know if you never ask.

Remember there are cognitive needs and differences between the way children process ideas and the procedure for adults. The education, vocabulary, maturity, exposure, etc. are different. Listen to Paul explain it. "When I was a child, I spake as a child, I understood as a child, I thought as a child: but when I became a man, I put away childish things."- I Corinthians 13:11

"Just because your children aren't responding to you doesn't always mean they aren't listening. It could be that the difference in your perspectives is so great that you sometimes might as well be living in different countries and speaking different languages. Learning to listen to *how* something is said instead of just the *words* that are said can help everyone communicate more effectively. It can literally make a world of difference!" – *The Way They Learn,* by Cynthia Tobias.

Remember that your students of all ages have taught themselves how they perceive or how they take in the information given. It determines their learning *style*. Your classroom will represent several learning styles, or how each learns best. That is why words alone are often an inadequate way to reach all of your students.

Be careful not to avoid questions from students. Questions shift my focus from all my notes and trying to rush through my notes to cover all the stuff, to focusing on the student. After all, you teach Joe and Sue and Sammy, and the Smith couple, or old man Johnson, not just the next lesson in your quarterly. ***The student's understanding is why you do not get upset when a question is asked.***

Talk for two hours if you want, but if they do not "get it," nothing is going to happen.

In conclusion, Step 2 is for this purpose: (1) To understand what this truth means. (2) We define words and terms, with illustrations. (3) We allow for questions and/or discussion, if needed. (4) We **assume nothing** concerning what they "should" know already. (5) The goal is for no student to proceed without a clear understanding.

Step 3 is To Personalize

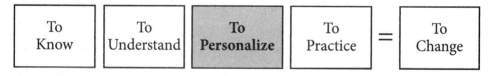

To Know	To Understand	**To Personalize**	To Practice	=	To Change

Let me preface this third step briefly. When we see the total Step process we look at it from two divisions. Step 1 and 2, To Know, To Understand, is all ***teacher centered.*** It is mainly the teacher who does most of the talking and clarification. The reason is, in most occasions, the student needs this introductory help. Most do not have a clue what the lesson is even about; thus, we start with Step 1. The teacher proceeds then with Step 2 or the understanding of words and terms. It is ***teacher centered*** in these first two steps because the teacher knows much more than the student knows. He/she prepares this "groundwork" for what is to come. That is why you studied all week while the student did not.

When we enter **Step 3,** the shift goes to ***student centered.*** Here is what is so often the problem. The teacher has convinced himself that if he gets through his nine pages of notes, that "surely they will get it." He could care less about the use of senses, questions, discussions, word studies, illustrations, role plays, etc. For to him, he has all the answers. "Just sit there and wait 'till I'm through. You'll get it, you'll get it!" And so goes another Sunday Bible class.

But, if this content alone goes on and on, it cancels out the student centered steps of 3 and 4. Student centered affords the only possibility for the lesson to transfer into life change.

An excellent book, ***Creative Bible Teaching* by Richards and Bredfeldt** states,

Teachers teach one big idea!

"Great teachers do not teach more; they tend to teach less with more focus. They teach one 'big idea.' They avoid the shotgun approach to teaching in favor of aiming with rifle accuracy. The greatest obstacle to effective teaching is not that we teach too little, but that we teach too much. Great teachers are focused."

Therefore, the goal for our total class time should be about 50% content and at least 50% application. Step 3 and 4 cannot happen in the last few moments of class. Getting to the student centered part of the process is why you teach. It holds the only possibility of life-change!

Now, let us get back to **Step 3.** The first step centered on the student and his personal life.

Once understood, God's truth must become God's truth to me. Now, it is God's truth, whether we believe it or not; we are not debating that. But, God's Word needs to strike home. This step helps the student to see himself in the lesson. It may be a lesson about Peter or Paul or John; but I see "me" in this truth!

When we establish the "<u>need to know</u>" the content, students will see a greater reason to know whatever the content may be. Personalizing brings truth closer to home. So, we compare it, contrast it, and give "at home" (local) illustrations. When you find yourself identifying with the truth, you will find your heart is stirred and your desire becomes an immediate need of your life!

Jesus was excellent in helping people to see themselves in the truth taught. Remember what happened in John 8:1-11. In verse 9 they saw themselves "being convicted in their own conscience," (the woman caught in adultery).

Personalizing brings truth closer to home.

To **personalize** demands we must know as much about our students as possible. When we know our students, it becomes easy to make up a hypothetical scenario that could easily fit the life style of those students. "What if this happened to you . . .?"

Personalizing the truth is the start that leads to life-changing decisions.

Findley B. Edge, in his book *Teaching for Results* says that *"the danger of leading the members to learn only verbalized concepts.* -This is a problem that confronts any type of education, but it is a particular problem in religious education because basically Christianity is an experience – an experience with Christ that must express itself in experience."

A **child's** world is not easily compared to the one in which you grew up in. Refresh yourself with the child's peer group, elementary schools, things that happen on playgrounds, cell phones in kid's pockets, play stations, and the latest doodads- gadgets- or gizmos available for children.

A **teen's** world is different too. Teens do not think the way you thought a few years ago. Get to know a teen's world of exposure and pressures. What do most like to watch on TV?

Even if you teach **adults** and are comparable in the same age bracket, you do not walk in their shoes. You do not have their personality, or problems. You were not raised by his parents, or been under her circumstances, or lived in his home. You do not have the unbelievable debt accumulated by the James family. You do not have two kids into drugs, or one child who is totally unmanageable. You have not gone for three years without a new dress, but Sue has. You have not been out of work for six months with no job in sight. Your first-born son is not in the war zone. You are different, and so are all the other students in that same class. **You must get to know them!**

Personalizing makes truth relevant to the real life of your students. In your week of preparation, work hard at this. Come to class ready to relate God's wonderful answers to real life – your student's real life! The learner must identify himself in God's truth for his personal life. That is why there must be adequate time for Step 3 in the process.

Somewhere in your lesson the truth has got to be brought out of Bible lands and times and customs, to today's lands and times and customs. What has that truth got to do with me? If I never see myself in that truth, there is no possibility for life-change.

So, Step 3 is for this purpose: (1) To **cause** the student to see himself in the truth. (2) We compare it, contrast it, give "at home" illustrations. (3) We prepare the heart to be stirred. (4) It is Step 3 in the process – A must!

What does that truth have to do with me?

Step 4 is To Practice

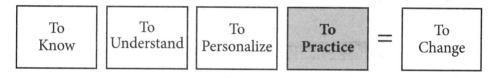

To Know	To Understand	To Personalize	To Practice	=	To Change

This step moves closer to life change as it illustrates what the truth looks like in real life. What does it look like in "street clothes"? What does that truth look like inside my house on Monday- Saturday, or between me and my wife, my kids, or my workplace? Tell me that!

God's Word is for changing lives! That is why I have to transition from teacher centered to student centered, with time enough to make all the above happen. If God's truth never gets into my life style, then perhaps learning has yet to take place.

Look again at the objective of the Word of God.

"All scripture is given by inspiration of God, and is profitable for doctrine, for reproof, for correction, for instruction in righteousness."
II Timothy 3:16

For This Purpose . . .

"That the man of God may be perfect, throughly furnished unto all good works."
II Timothy 3:17

God's wonderful Word, all of it, is given for doctrine, reproof, correction, instruction in righteousness, for the purpose of verse 17.

Therefore, with whatever Scripture you use in class, it has unbelievable potential, and God is willing to develop it in your students. That is why you teach! That is why you refuse to give another long dose of content and expect the student to go home and change his life.

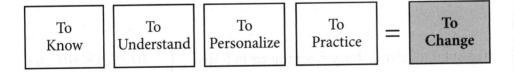

| To Know | To Understand | To Personalize | To Practice | = | **To Change** |

Step 5 is To Change

Within the final and ultimate Step in the process lies the possibility of **life-change!** The teacher can do all of the above, say their little prayer at the end, "You know folks, we all ought to live like that," and dismiss the class. If so, it will be class as usual, with little to no possibility of life-change. But, we do not have to!

For example, earlier I used an illustration of "surrender of life" as my lesson. Now, with five minutes left (the Big 5), here is how I would end my class.

"Class, God has been helping us to see what it really means to surrender all to Him. For forty minutes now, God has tried to make this truth crystal clear. He asked each one of us if we are willing to **be** anything He would want us to be? Are we willing to **do** anything God would ever ask us to do? Are we willing to **go** anywhere He would ever ask us to go? Now, He is waiting for our response. Class, we have four or five minutes left. Would you just bow your head right now and give the dear Lord your response. Have you ever really surrendered all to your Lord? And if not, would you like to right now?"

Here is the place you stop talking and allow God to work on the inside. Have a short testimony time after their prayers! You give a twenty second testimony of how this lesson helped you during the week, to get it started.

Do you see the significance of the process that leads us to this end? Think for a moment about each step, and the consequences of leaving one step out, or of giving thirty-five minutes to Steps 1-2, and five minutes to Steps 3-4.

> *Stop talking and allow God to work on the inside.*

In addition to the Learning Process that helps us greatly to stay on course and is our opportunity to see life change take place, there is more!

The **passion** and **compassion** of the teacher will mean so much as the words come along. The teacher's mannerisms add up to 93% of communication (what actually comes across.)

> **Passion, or the lack thereof, is so often the difference in success, mediocrity, or failure.**

The mandate is for the teacher to improve to their maximum ability.

"To say 'I don't need to prepare,' demeans the event and over-values your skills. Every event in life is worth the time it takes to polish the details." *The Encore Effect* by Mark Sanborn.

The event you prepare for far exceeds others – as you prepare to teach God's Word! Passion comes from your "*wanter.*" Your heart, your spirit, your great desire to be a teacher for God will push yourself to always be well prepared!

"The teacher is the intermediary of the message. He stands between the Lord and the people. He is the delivery mechanism that the Lord gave to the church. The teacher of God is the living link between the Word of God and the people of God." – *The Seven Laws of the Learner,* by Bruce Wilkinson.

If teaching a Bible class is the largest effort you give for your Lord, then surely you would want to get better and better! Why would I drift into spending less preparation time, less reading of books that would help me, less trying of new methods and techniques, and less prayer for my students? Surely, as your time to meet God grows closer, your effort to serve Him through teaching would grow stronger! "Thank you, dear Lord, for the opportunity to be the one person in the classroom to make all of this happen!"

Principles Of Planning Your Lesson Will Always Help You!

Write down your plan. When I spend time writing down my ideas I can now see them, the sequence, the natural progression as God so often lays it out for us in His Word. I write it, I see it, I rehearse it again in my mind as I go through the process. Without plans, without steps, it is often hard to arrive at a conclusion. Your class lesson cannot seem like a speaker who repeats himself over and over as if he is trying to find a runway to land on. You must know before you begin what your destination is to be. The process or the plan for your lesson will then get you there step by step. Steps will keep you on track, steps will give you assurance. The steps of the Learning Process will go a long way to keeping you on track! That is how I prepare my lesson.

Brian Tracy, in his book, **Time Power** states, "*Resist the tendency toward perfectionism. Since perfectionism is a major reason for procrastination, decide not to worry about doing the job perfectly. Just get started and work steadily.*"

In the chapter on **Lesson Preparation**, we will make more suggestions for your weekly preparation. Refuse to live the life of a teacher in "neutral." Put your study into high gear and have the greatest year of preparedness ever!

6. Out-Achieve Yourself As A Teacher

Before we leave this chapter, let me share a thought that has always stirred me to try improving myself, with no end in sight. Here is the idea: **Out-Achieving Myself Is The Best Comparison!**

What is possible for you to achieve? In your role as teacher, how much better could you be than you are now? Exclude all the *"buts or ifs or maybes,"* and assume it is simply up to you to learn and apply what you learn – how much better could you be in one year? Without all the preconceived thoughts of what you could never achieve, but with the thought of reaching your highest dream, what would that dream be?

> *"Resist the tendency toward perfectionism."*

Just make your dream a big dream for you. Do not compare your big dream with someone else's dream; just make it yours! Start with you. What area of teaching do you presently feel very inadequate in? Could you read one of the best books to teach yourself how to study and find things in your own Bible? Could you remind yourself of the characteristics of your age group in the next six weeks? Could you purchase or make a new visual to enhance your teaching? Could you rejuvenate your classroom in the next three months? Make your list. Prioritize your list, and start with the first one. Set a *deadline* for the first goal. Then, go to the next. **Out-achieve yourself!**

The Scriptures give us forty verses in one chapter of one book, after hundreds of other verses given, just to illustrate that any and all people can have faith (Hebrews 11:1-40). Set your goal by faith to out-achieve yourself!

Back in the "hills" there was a high achiever, a kinda "thick" little woman named Elsie Toots. At a local town fair Elsie came out the winner of the Chocolate Eating Contest again for the seventh straight year. Elsie was given the Consolidated Chocolate Makers of America award as "Sweetheart of the Year." She finished off twelve large boxes of chocolates in only fourteen minutes and twelve seconds! It took six men to wheel her off the platform, but the whole town had a proud moment. That is what I am saying, do something really big for you!

As you think, so goes your teaching ministry!

I believe the greater motivation is not another person, but it **lies within yourself.** If I can see myself growing in knowledge, wisdom, understanding, and my skills are sharper than ever before, then out-achieving myself is the better comparison. The circumstances, personal finances, past experiences, facilities, etc., may not be an accurate picture with which to compare yourself to someone else. Your goal must be the best **you** can achieve, but *nothing less than your personal best!* You always know when you are giving your best, both in preparation and in presentation. You know.

It would be a great thing to list ten areas of teaching in which you could consider improving yourself. Try one to get started.

What was my original purpose? Is this still in tact? If not, why not? How is my efficiency each week? Where do I lose or waste time? Can I out-achieve my goals of last year? How is my time management? What effort is given to discipleship of my students? Out-achieving myself brings great rewards.

Harvey S. Firestone said, **"Accept no one's definition of your life, but define yourself."**

"Without fail, when you embrace this 'why me' attitude, the victim mentality will paralyze your attitude and your enthusiasm," *says David Cottrell,* in his book **Monday Morning Choices.** Forget the higher education of someone else, the twenty years of experience of some other teacher over you, of the church training that other teachers have had and you have not. Start where you are, and spend the rest of your life getting better in every area of teaching you can list. God knows your past. He knows that leadership has never provided training for teachers. That may never change, but you can change!

7. The Blame Game Is Not For A Teacher

The blame game is not good. When you **own** your goal set, you then own the victories or the losses. But that is fine, for no one is perfect anyway. You will ultimately be the one to decide that you will have the attitude of an achiever or a loser. You must be in control of your choices.

For over thirty-five years I have traveled this nation, trying to help our Churches to train their teachers. It is pathetic. We turn over the teaching of God's Word to a lay teacher who has never received training. We do not even teach them how to get more out of their own Bible study. They go for years like that, as leadership "assumes" that all is fine. However, leadership has never heard their teachers teach. We assume because they have a good personality, or because she is married to a deacon that she should make a good teacher. WRONG!

> *You must be in control of your choices.*

For example, the last five meetings I have conducted, there were thirty-five churches who brought their teachers to attend. Out of the thirty-five churches attending, thirty-three had **never ever** had any type of training whatsoever in **thirty years.** I know how bad it is, for thirty-five years I have asked the teachers who come. It is always the same. But that still does not give me the "out" to just blame my circumstances on someone else.

I do not have to go a day longer without what others have had. Check out our aids available to you at *TrainingTeachers.org.* Get a hold of something that will help you today and begin.

Your personal attitude will be a major part of out-achieving yourself. Without the proper attitude or out-look, achievement goals will be rare in your life. You need the right attitude to give you that *push* that will be there to help you out-achieve yourself.

Attitudes give testimony to the deep-down beliefs you hold. Without this strong passionate *push* from within, the drive to excel will not be enough. The drive supersedes any pep talk your pastor can give or any "self-talk" you can do for yourself.

In the Christian's world our key word is *faith*. Faith is above and beyond my ability to accomplish within myself or by my own resources. If I have the ability to accomplish the task, then do it. If I need it, and have the resources for it, then go ahead and get it. I do not need faith for what I can see, but I do for what I cannot see.

Faith comes in when it is above and beyond my ability or my resources. So, what is on my list that I must trust God for? Faith trusts the Lord to bring it to pass, as I trust Him for it. Thus, I can trust God to actually do far and above that which I could ever do. Again, it all comes from deep down inside, from the heart of men and women.

Faith or believing God is for us to take advantage of throughout our lifetime, and available upon request. "Jesus answered and said unto them, Verily I say unto you, If ye have faith, and doubt not, ye shall not only do this which is done to the fig tree, but also if ye shall say unto this mountain, Be thou removed, and be thou cast into the sea; it shall be done. And all things, whatsoever ye shall ask in prayer, believing, ye shall receive." Matthew 21:21-22

"It is difficult if not impossible to be remarkable at doing something you don't have your heart in." Mark Sanborn, Encore Effect

We, therefore, can do above and beyond our highest dreams to date. With that attitude, we are willing to tackle that giant-size dream! We can out-achieve our best teaching thus far. With God, my abilities can soar to out-achieve anything I have ever attempted before! If it takes a newly developed skill, I can develop that skill.

Again, in the book ***Monday Morning Choices***, we read, **"The choice of persistence is about setting a goal and reaching it, about coming to roadblocks and hurdling them, about continuing the journey in spite of life's speed bumps."**

What an excellent thought! I do not want to go through life with no desire to accomplish more than to date. I cannot live on yesterday's goals and accomplishments. That time of fulfillment lasted for the moment, but the moment is long gone.

> *We can do above and beyond our highest dreams to date.*

"No one plans to become mediocre. Rather, mediocrity is the result of no plan at all." Tom Newberry, *Success Is Not An Accident*

It seems so logical to be able to out-achieve yourself. Take your last big project or your last best lesson, and consider this: (1) What were the best parts of the lesson? (2) Where did the lesson bog down? Why? How can I avoid that next time? (3) How could I get to my main thought faster in order to spend maximum time on the major thought? (4)With brainstorming for new ideas, my teacher-friends could help me to see an even better approach. (5) Could I take the most experienced teacher in our church out to lunch, to glean what he/she knows that I do not know?

Now I have increased my wisdom, knowledge, and understanding of teaching!

Could I not expect to out-achieve myself next time? Sure, unless my attitude had already taken me down failure lane and I am ready to quit. This world is over saturated with quitters and under-achievers. Let every book you read, every new technique you try, every evaluation *push you* to the next accomplishment!

What an unusual opportunity God has given to you. Then think of the heavy-duty responsibility of being a teacher for God! Such a privilege is given to a few. Our goal is far greater than going to be with our God someday as a "mediocre" or as a "less than my best" teacher.

A great little book for motivation and inspiration is the book **The Lombardi Rules** by Vince Lombardi, Jr. He says, "Aim for the stars: When people are encouraged to reach beyond their grasp, the results can be eye-opening. Successful leaders don't buy into perceived limitations."

As you teach, you become much like a "coach." You inform as to the right action for the student to take, and you seek to inspire the student to reach higher goals than ever before. I believe that everyone, deep down, wants to out-achieve themselves.

Always reminding your students of the greatness of someone else may actually "not" inspire your students. Out-achieving yourself is an easier pill to swallow. Develop yourself, and they will see the value of themselves.

> **Enthusiasm is felt, seen, heard, and remembered for years to come. Share your enthusiasm.**

The goal you wish for students to reach must be reachable. When students are inspired to reach for more, we must give them not just the *what*, but the *why*!

Even as a high school kid playing football, I understood that the closer you got to the end zone, the whole team's perfection had to increase, because so did the opponent's. The field of perfection now had been reduced, not with 100 yards of playing field, but now to only 10 yards of field.

As a teacher, as in football, *striving* will get you there. Anything less will lower your expectations, and thus your efforts. Your striving may have gotten you 98 yards down the field, but there are still 2 yards to go to score. *Preparation* is striving. For the teacher, *praying* is striving. *Execution* is striving. Crossing the goal line will need an extra surge of striving. "I press toward the mark," that is the goal of the teacher, in order to see the students follow you into the end zone!

May God help us to put so much heart and labor into our work for God, that we would walk away from one Sunday class with this thought ringing in our mind, *"I can't wait 'till next Sunday morning!"* Do you feel that way after your class has ended? Have you ever felt that way? Why not? What else do you do that has the level of significance as the teaching of God's Word?

Now, practice this attitude: *"I can't wait for the next chapter of this book!"*

A Review Of Key Thoughts:

1. Can you repeat the parts labeled as the Learning Process?

2. Why is To Personalize so significant for a teacher to plan for? _____

_____

_____

3. We used a quote worth remembering: "No one plans to become mediocre.

Rather, mediocrity is the result of _____ _____

at all." From the book *Success Is Not An Accident.*

4. What does it mean in Step 2 of the Learning Process, TO UNDERSTAND?

_____

_____

_____

Chapter THREE

The Greater Purpose In Teaching: Life Change!

Why could we teach for twenty years and never (as far as we can tell) see change in our students from our teaching? I believe there is a reason. Then, how do we see change before the bell rings?

Life change is the whole reason for God's Word, and it is the reason we teach!

III. The Greater Purpose In Teaching: Life Change!

1. Why Can't We See Results Before We Say "Class Dismissed"?

2. Content Alone Does Not Change Lives, Without Application

3. The End Should Really Be The Beginning!

4. The "Big Five" Should Be Big On Your List

5. An Example Of Passing Up An Opportunity

6. Causing The Student To Learn

7. It Brings A Driving Urgency To Prepare Well

8. "Ya' Ought To" Is Not Enough Urgency

9. What Does This Truth Look Like Inside My House?

III. The Greater Purpose In Teaching: Life Change!

Teaching a class to actually see life change before the teacher says "class dismissed" is like a foreign concept in our churches today. I say that, because even if we confess to agreeing with life change as the goal, in practicality it could not possibly happen. *We do not allow it to happen.*

1. Why Can't We See Results Before We Say "Class Dismissed"?

How is it that we can teach a class of children, teens, or adults for twenty-five years, and not one time ever see a person's life changed in our classroom? Why? *Because we do not allow it to happen.* Let me explain.

Why is it that when Pastor preaches a message in church, then at the "official church invitation" people come forward, bowing before the Lord? They are there to put aside sin or add a great value to their life. In other words, *when they had that few minutes of time to "face God" about the issue, their life changed!*

But, wait a minute. Six weeks ago we thoroughly taught the same thing in Sunday School and "nothing happened." What made the difference? Is that the difference in preaching and teaching? Is the Pastor just that much better in clarifying truth than all of us teachers? I do not get it.

Let us compare what Pastor did to what we did as a teacher:

(1) Pastor studied and prayed all week.
(2) Pastor clarified words and gave application well.
(3) Pastor poured out his heart in giving the message.
(4) At the end, Pastor gave an invitation (actually he turns us over to God.)
(5) People came to respond to God and lives changed!

Now, let us see how our Sunday School hour compares:

(1) Teacher studied and prayed all week. (same)
(2) Teacher clarified words and gave application well. (same)
(3) Teacher poured out his heart in giving the message. (same)
(4) At the end, the teacher said, "We all ought to live like that." (different)
(5) We had a quick prayer and dismissed, but nothing changed. (different)

Could we say there is a difference in numbers (4) and (5)?

I firmly believe that is where the difference lies. Pastor **gives people time** to respond to God about the truth just heard. The Sunday School teacher allows for **no such time.**

We all know that when a spiritual change takes place it all comes down to **just me and just God.** But, without my time to respond to Him it is only another reminder that "I ought to" someday.

The difference is what we refer to as an invitation. *Pastor always gives one* in church; *we never give one* in Sunday School. An invitation is simply a response time to God (where spiritual transformations take place).

2. Content Alone Does Not Change Lives Without Application

Somewhere in the past years the Sunday School settled for more content and less application, which would not take long for the teacher's expectations of life change to dwindle. Teachers now are expecting the content they give to change student's lives. That is why they arrive with such a massive dose of words to say.

> *Teachers now are expecting the content they give to change students' lives.*

However, unless content is thoroughly illustrated through clear application into real life, it will not change lives. Perhaps it can make us more knowledgeable of God's Word. However, it is too often in knowledge only, but not in living. So, the question is, will it ever change in your class?

3. The End Should Really Be The Beginning!

There has to be a time before the bell rings that *God has time to work within the heart.* If that time never happens, then do not expect spiritual results to come along later in the week.

This time means you must discipline yourself to stop talking. Plan it into your notes. Your goal is to get them to the point where you can turn your students over to God. Their life, at least in one area, could change immediately.

I illustrated earlier how to conclude the lesson. No, you do not have to sing a song, just a time to immediately respond to the Lord. Sometimes, I may only hand out a 3x5 card, asking my students to write a one sentence prayer to God, as their response to His truth. Keep it in your Bible for several weeks. Every time you open your Bible, it reminds you of what you said to God.

Think through the goal you have for the lesson you have, then, tailor the response that seems appropriate. ***The idea is to not overlook the response time.***

Let me add this thought: It is not that we must begin to give an invitation every week in our class. But why did you teach that lesson? We must stop assuming that if students hear the truth, some will go home and get on their knees before God and their life will change. Do not spend your life waiting for that to happen. When is the last time it happened to one of your students?

It is not that we are insincere about life change, but our passion for change has settled for just teaching instead of ***compelling*** and ***persuading*** and ***encouraging*** them to act on the truth. Remember, your students are only one prayer away from making everything right with God! This could happen before they get out of their chair in your classroom, ***but not without the opportunity.***

Even church people can be controlled by Satan, not possessed, but controlled, as with Ananias and Sapphira (Acts 5:1-3). The anticipation of life change changes your week of preparation, your prayer time, and your hour of presentation. There is a greater urgency that life change might happen on next Sunday!

4. The "Big Five" Should Be Big On Your List

You do not have to give an invitation every week. You do not have to sing sixteen verses of "Just As I Am" until the whole class takes one giant step forward for God. To me, I call it the "Big Five." I put that at

> *If not careful, I can keep on talking until there is no time left for God.*

the bottom of my lesson or message notes. This reminds me to be careful with my time and to allow at least five minutes at the end **when I stop talking**. Who ever heard of a teacher who stopped talking before time was up?

The reason for at least five minutes is that I am now going to turn over my students and myself to God! It is now time for the Spirit of God to work on the inside- which is not my realm at all. God works on the heart. If not careful, I can keep on talking until there is no time left for God.

If your Pastor did not give an invitation, it would be the talk of the church. Everyone expects it. That is when people get saved, rededicate themselves to serve the dear Lord, to get something out or put something into their life. It is simply a time set aside to respond to God in your own heart about the truth just heard.

So, the question returns again, **why do we never do that in Sunday School** *or Bible Class?*

Here is another thought: Some of the very best lessons or messages given this year are in your Bible class, not necessarily from the pulpit. Hang on, I am not degrading the pulpit or preaching. Your Pastor has the whole Bible to preach. He has plenty to preach about besides what you are teaching this week or this whole month.

I am just saying that the specific area of real life that you will teach for the next 2-3 weeks, Pastor may not even cover for six months. Remember that he has the whole Bible to preach.

5. An Example Of Passing Up An Opportunity

Let me give an example. Your lesson deals with "Surrender Of Life," what does that really mean? Pastor does not plan to go there for six months or so. In your classroom, if you knew their hearts, there are fourteen out of twenty students who have never surrendered all to Christ. They know it, and God knows it.

> *Could your student surrender all to Christ while still in your classroom?*

Students have heard many times from you and from Pastor that to be in God's will, surrender of life is demanded. These students have come already knowing they "ought to" surrender all, but never have. In fact, they know and God knows what it is they refuse to surrender. So, here they sit in your classroom!

If the situation is "normal," they will hear again that they "ought to surrender." They will hear "how to surrender all" as you teach. Now, the class comes down to the last five minutes of time. If there is not a response time, the student will walk back out the door the same way he came in.

However, if the teacher will allow for a response time, then there is nothing to do but to jump into the arms of Jesus! Could your students surrender all to Christ while still in your classroom? Sure they can, **if they have time** to say "Yes" to Jesus! If not, the cycle continues.

So, the idea is not a suggestion for a mandatory "invitation" each week of class. The idea is to allow that "*Big Five*" response time when the lesson leans in that direction. Try it one time!

Here is my final thought. To prove to you how quickly your lesson takes a nose dive once you say class dismissed, watch for this: Within ten seconds after you say, "Class dismissed," everyone in the class is talking about something entirely different than what has been pouring out of your heart for the last forty minutes. Watch it. The truth just flies away in ten seconds and nothing happens.

6. Causing The Student To Learn

The ultimate objective of life change demands the higher level of learning to be reached in time to **Personalize** the truth and to see how to **Practice** the truth in life.

Bruce Wilkinson in *The Seven Laws Of The Learner* warns us with a couple of thoughts: "Teachers have separated themselves from their students and redefined teaching as what the teacher says rather than what the student learns. . . .They think about teaching as what they do – their focus is upon themselves. Many teachers cover their material and leave the room thinking they have taught."

Our role is to *cause* students to learn. That may put a lot of teachers on a guilt trip, ready to give up and do something else. However, there is a very bright side that should help us to jump for joy.

The glorious side of teaching is that if God has led you in that direction, that of teaching, His promises are almost endless that He will help you!

For example, I may think I am not creative enough to cause students to learn, like other teachers. But, when I educate myself I can become extremely creative.

I must remember that this is the Lord's church, it is His students, it is His Word you teach. We can rest in the truth that He wants us and our classroom to be as creative as need be. The church should be the most creative force on earth! Remember *Who* is on your side! It was God who walked out on the edge of *nothing* and created *all things*. Remember Him? Do you think He is not willing to help you become the creative teacher that He needs for that room? He is there for you!

7. It Brings A Driving Urgency To Prepare Well

My goal now becomes greater than to "just get by next week." To prepare myself well immediately means to start early in the week in my preparation. Over these four decades of church ministry I have seen the week of preparation decline and become less urgent than it used to have been. The time alone has gone from five hours to four, to three, to two, and it is not uncommon for teachers to admit they spend only one hour on next week's lesson. I sure hope they do not teach my grand children.

But wait a minute, this is God, it is His church; and yet there is no urgency in sight. How much more motivation do we need? One of the greatest roles to perform in a local church is teaching. I could not think of a greater role to play for a lay person in a church.

One more time, remember the teacher's objective: "*To so clarify what God has to say to the student, that the student could not possibly miss what God has to say to him.*"

I will never understand how God could choose someone like you or me to be responsible for carrying out such a huge goal. But, He has given that role to us. We cannot forget that at the judgment seat of Christ, He will bring it up again.

Bring what up? The *stewardship* we gave the ministry He gave to us will come into question.

That is another reason why I must have a strong desire to improve myself more and more each year!

8. "Ya' Ought To" Is Not Enough Urgency.

This backwoods country phrase worked well as I grew up in the mountains of Tennessee. For example, instead of saying, "Hey, Buster, we are thinking about going to the fair. Would you like to go with us?" In the backwoods, we would just say, "Goin' fair – y'ont to?" Why, that took out thirteen words you did not have to say!

But, "Y'ont to?" or "Ya' ought to" is not clear enough for a teacher of God's Word. I must have the clearest definitions and the most recognizable illustrations when I handle God's Word. ***Truths that last for eternity are said in your classroom!***

Truths that last for eternity are said in your classroom!

To finish your lesson and close with a simple, "You know folks, we all ought to. . ." is not good enough. Have you told them HOW to? If so, now give them the opportunity to do so!

"Ya' ought to" gives the thought that someday "ya' ought to" get around to giving this area of your life to God. Those type of instructions fade quickly away. There is no urgency in "someday."

Urgency means there will be tears of compassion for your students during your week of preparation. You cannot but suggest, persuade, or compel them to do what God is asking them to do!

Do you come across as though you really do believe what you teach? Could I give testimony of this truth in my own life, or am I just another "talking head"? Am I just saying what I am expected to say, or is there a great sense of urgency? Can my students hear it in my voice? Can they see it in my facial expressions? Does the teacher believe this stuff?

Do you prepare and present with much expectation or anticipation of life change? It is no more "ya' ought to," but you must and you can right now before our class is finished. Your mannerisms will follow those feelings of high expectations. Thus, you will teach as one who believes the words he says!

"The Bible wasn't given for our information but for our transformation." – D.L. Moody

9. What Does This Truth Look Like Inside My House?

You are teaching students who live their lives outside of your classroom, where real life stuff takes place. Your classroom is an hour at best. There are 144 other hours to be lived that are outside the range of your voice each week. Will they be clear enough on the truth you taught to remember it when it shows up in real life?

That again is how significant your role is. God has graciously bestowed upon you the privilege to be a key to your students' spiritual growth. That is one of those *Wow!* things you get to prepare for!

As you prepare your lesson and as you pray your way through the week, that is when you pray by name and by need. Visit your students. Find out the atmosphere inside their house. You need knowledge and wisdom for each student. You do not gain that sitting at home and wondering.

You need a clue that helps you relate the lesson to real life- their real life!

The more you know about your students gives you added knowledge. Now you can plan your lesson in light of who you teach. If not, then just teach anything, because they probably need it anyway. You need a clue that helps you relate the lesson to real life-their real life!

The goal is to be so practical that the students see themselves in that truth *(To Personalize)*. The **child** sees that truth lived out on the playground at school. The **teenagers** see how to avoid the pitfalls of gossip, or lying, or bullying, or the quicksand of the internet. The **adult** can see how that truth fits the "season of life" they find themselves in.

What does that truth look like in street clothes, on the sidewalk, in the business world, or inside my house? Tell me that. Tell me what truth looks like!

Throughout the New Testament we read over and over how Paul wrote the Word of God to meet needs. Just a handful include anger, immorality, lawsuits, gossip, rebuke, the poor, gluttony, drunkenness, rudeness, deceit, self-exaltation, patience, and page after page of more needs common to people living real lives.

In your class, students are all dressed up, carrying their Bible, answering Bible questions, singing praises to God, and yet have deep seated-needs. Some "church folks" when back home are lying, cheating, stealing, into drugs, alcohol, watching shows like MTV, HBO, or others. Some church folks are into "private" pornography, an affair, thinking about leaving the church, social drinking, dating the unsaved, doubting the Bible, disobedient to parents, and the list goes on.

As teacher, you cannot make people clean up their act. But, in your class, you will give the truth in love, but you will give the truth with great clarity. They will know in your class that they could learn if they would learn.

Remember that your work is similar to that of Christ in this respect: When Jesus walked this earth, He would teach a man truth close-up and personal. But when He finished, that man walked away in unbelief; and Jesus was the teacher. It shows us that we humans have all the capacity to look the Son of God in the face and "spit" on Him. That is what we are capable of doing. Sometimes the nod of the head in agreement with you or the occasional "Amen" does not really carry much belief behind them. So, as teacher, I cannot look at my class as committers of all the above, but understand that Christ faced every student that you face today.

Hypocrisy is pretending to be something or someone that we ourselves know we are not. The original languages call this type person an *actor* or one who *wears a mask.* **Luke 20:20, "And they watched him, and sent forth spies, which should feign (pretend) themselves just men, that they might take hold of his words, that so they might deliver him unto the power and authority of the governor."** Paul even accused Peter of hypocrisy in Galatians 2. Even the upright Barnabas was led to stray.

Remember the eye-opening passage of Paul on Mars Hill: Acts 17:32-34, **"And when they heard of the resurrection of the dead, some mocked: and others said, We will hear thee again of this matter. Vs. 33 So Paul departed from among them. Vs. 34 Howbeit certain men clave unto him, and believed."** Here is the potential for every class you teach: *some* mocked, *some* said we will hear more, *some* believed!

So, prepare well to make sure no student misunderstands or misinterprets what the Lord is saying. Pray well for each student by name and by need. As teacher, you cannot make people clean up their act. But, in your classroom they could learn if they would learn, and they could turn from any sin if the need is there.

There is a must read book for all teachers, ***Already Gone*** by **Ham &Beemer.** Ham is the creationist we all know. This book shows us a study of 1,000 former church students, now in their twenties, solidly raised in the church but no longer attending, with no intentions of returning, and their reasons why. This study is with students like yours in your fundamental church, none were from "liberal" churches. "The spiraling descent can be described in one word: ***IRRELEVANCE***. . .The root of the word 'relevance' comes from the word 'relate.' In order for something to be relevant, it has to connect (or relate) to something that is real and important. The problem we are studying, of course, is that 60 percent of the students who grow up in the Church have lost that connection."

So, that is why I am trying to fill your mind with the need to **apply** your lesson far more than you keep adding more and more content. Church folks are filled to the brim with content. They

> *"The spiraling descent can be described in one word: IRRELEVANCE"*

have already heard 2,000 lessons, and 3,000 sermons, and a multitude of lessons over and over again; and they still do not get it. The evidence is seen in their life or their home and family.

However, the truth of God is far superior to any temptation that will come our way. In my classroom, my great goal is that my students will not miss what God has to say to them about their everyday real life.

We must give teaching our priority interest. Wesley Willis in ***Make Your Teaching Count***, says, "Sitting in a classroom under a teacher's poorly designed instruction. . . People don't hate learning. . .Learning is unpleasant only if it seems useless or irrelevant."

Let me remind you again of this wonderful thought: ***"You are never more than one prayer away from making everything right with God."*** Wow! That is why you teach and that is why you compel and persuade, and with great compassion allow time for your students to respond to God about that truth you have prepared to teach all week long! Anticipate great results from the teaching of God's Word! That is why the Lord asked you to teach. How about another ***Wow!***

A Review Of Key Thoughts:

1. We often see no response in class because we do not allow it. How do we

not allow it? _____

_____

2. Have you gone for years in teaching to see no actual decisions made in the

classroom? How could it change? _____

_____

_____

3. Compare your end of class lesson with pastor's end of preaching. What is

the difference? _____

_____

4. Finish: Pastor gives people time to respond to God about the truth just

heard. The Sunday School _____.

5. Define what was meant by the "Big Five."

_____

_____

6. Within ten seconds after the teacher says "class dismissed," the whole class

is doing what? _____

_____

7. One of the best thoughts is this: "People don't hate learning. .

.Learning is unpleasant only if it seems _____ or

_____."

Chapter FOUR

The Teacher's Week Of Preparation

The Week of Preparation! It is where you plan to see great success on Sunday. Guidelines are here to help you begin early in the week, to organize your lesson, to choose less content than more, to get to your main thought quickly, to eliminate the peripheral content, to clarify your words and terms, to teach the way students learn best, and to "master" your lesson from seven pages of notes to a half-page.

That may be a very long sentence, but that is the goal of this chapter!

IV. The Teacher's Week Of Preparation

1. Allow Yourself More Time, Not Less

2. Start Early In The Week

3. Organizing Your Lesson

4. Remember, You Teach People, Not Lessons

5. Choose Less Content, But The Best Content

6. Getting To The Precise Target Quickly

7. Mash The Delete Button To Eliminate Time Absorbers

8. Too Much Is Often Just Too Much

9. You Have A Mandate When You Teach!

10. Master Your Lesson (A Key To Communication)!

11. Clarifying God's Truth Leads To Changing Lives!

12. Including All Students In Ways They Each Learn Best!

13. Focus Keeps You On Target!

IV. The Teacher's Week Of Preparation

1. Allow Yourself More Time, Not Less

Teachers have different innate abilities, experiences, formal training or lack of, personal initiative, and an attitude. You should take stock of your own to personally evaluate where you are and where you need improvement.

It may take you a total of five hours each week to prepare yourself well to teach. If that is what it takes for you, never cut yourself short of preparation time. The same lesson for a similar age level may take a teacher friend only three hours of preparation. You are your own example, not another teacher.

If you desire to be your very best for God as a teacher, *you will know* if you had adequate time for preparation. You may have a "gut" feeling on your way to church that you are not ready. You can feel it, and it is not a good feeling. Halfway through your lesson the feeling gets worse. When your lesson is finished you feel like crying. Perhaps you should. Learn fast to commit the proper time that you need. *God will honor your effort.*

"Self-discipline is the ability to do what you should do, when you should do it, whether you feel like it or not." *No Excuses* by Brian Tracy

2. Start Early In The Week

Let us lay out first a *progression schedule* to guide us through the week. Later on we will deal with allowing the Holy Spirit to guide you throughout your week of preparation.

Here, let us think through a plan of putting our lesson together, step by step, as the week progresses. You will see here the idea to start early in the week, rather than at the end of the week. In this schedule by Friday, you have only spent 2 ½ hours on your lesson, but it has now been on your mind all week. Now, the Spirit of God has something to work with- you!

Sunday Afternoon: (10 min.)

(1) Read the key passage for next week. (2) Ask the Spirit of God for illumination.

Sunday Night: (10 min.)

(1) Before bedtime, read the passage again.

Monday Morning: (10 min.)

(1) As part of your devotion time, reread the passage again. (2) Ask God to show you this truth in real life this week.

Monday Night: (25 min.)

(1) Read through the full passage. Begin selecting the one-line key thought that will be your objective on Sunday. Say it over to yourself several times. (2) Ask God for specific illustrations to clarify this truth to include both a Bible example and one in today's real life.

Tuesday Morning: (10 min.)

(1) Read your one-line key thought. (2) Ask God to remind you throughout the day of how to apply the truth to at least 3-4 of your students.

Tuesday Night: (20 min.)

(1) Read your objective again. Quote it to yourself. Apply it to another three of your students. Start making your notes to apply to each student.

Wednesday Morning: (10 min.)

(1) Read the passage again. Ask for God's blessings. (2) Think your way through the day with your key objective in mind. Ask God to give you a great fresh illustration to this truth.

Wednesday Night: (20 min.)

(1) Before or after church, try to write down two or three ways to illustrate the truth or a personal illustration. Give some form to your lesson direction.

Thursday Morning: (10 min.)

(1) Read the main objective. (2) Pray for each student by name. (3) Ask God to help you this weekend as you study. (4) Pray short prayers throughout the day for God's blessing.

Thursday Night: (30 min.)

(1) Now, for the specifics. Your study and your prayers must become more intense. (2) Pick out your final selection of content. Skim aside the rest. (3) Arrange content in the most logical order. Add in your illustrations where appropriate. (4) Review quickly your *Discipleship Roll Book* and your prayer list. Refresh your mind for this lesson and your students!

Friday Morning: (10 min.)

(1) Check once again for *logical order*. Does one step lead to the next? (2) Briefly list your major thoughts in their logical order on a card to carry with you today. Every hour or so, scan quickly the card for memory. (3) Pray for

God's blessing on Sunday!

Friday Night: (40 min.)

(1) Settle your decision on illustrations, visuals, and again your major objective (the one-line key thought). (2) Are your steps (1,2,3) in logical order that will lead to a clear understanding of your objective? Bring it to your irreducible minimum of steps. (3) Now, add in a 2-3 word summary of your methods and techniques for getting each step across (questions, readings, illustrations of real life, discussion, marker board, visual, etc.). (4) Complete your skeleton outline. Eliminate what you can. Read it again.

Saturday Morning: (90 min.)

(1) Ask God to clarify and affirm your lesson to you. (2) Go over each point or step of the lesson. Have you made your list of 2-3 word summaries of what comes next? (3) Read over your outline to see if you remember what the 2-3 word summary means. Your goal is that when you glance at the 2-3 word reminder of what comes next, your eyes quickly refocus on your students! (4) Pray again, specifically for your students, *by name.* (5) Ask God to help you to "master" your lesson and to empower you! (6) Are all your visuals ready and in proper order?

Saturday Night: (15 min.)

(1) Before bed time, read your reminder list again. Fix the logical order in your mind. (2) Ask God to seal this truth in your mind for tomorrow!

Sunday Morning: (15 min.)

(1) Up early. Go to God early. (2) Review your outline. (3) Somewhere, before class begins, find a closet or secret place to have a "self talk," just you and just God. Remind yourself again that life change could take place in your classroom today before the bell rings. (4) Now, you are ready to teach your heart out. One last time remind yourself that 93% of what comes across is by HOW you say what you say. *Where is the passion for teaching and the compassion for students?*

The *Teacher's Quick Reference Guide* may be of good help as you search for classroom involvement ideas, definitions of often used Bible words, visual techniques, dealing with children about salvation, counseling children, or dealing with good or bad character traits. See this binder on *TrainingTeachers.org.*

Let Us Summarize: This is an idea of organizing your time throughout the week. There is no "sacred cow" here, just a thought. However, over the years you have surely found yourself putting off and putting off your "so-called scheduled study time" for something that always comes up during the week. The schedule above is to help you consider *spreading out your time* throughout the week, in order to not have to "cram" as for a school test.

The listing above covers a bit over five hours of preparation time. If you spend two hours now, think of how better prepared you will be with one, two, or three hours more per week. It is "whatever" it takes for you. And you will be different than someone else. So, there is no hard and fast rule of time. But you should know. You

Never give less than your best to our Lord.

should be able to feel the adequate preparation or the inadequate study from within, even before class begins. Never give less than your very best to our Lord and to the Word of God!

Here is a tough statement, but I think a fair one: If you always feel like you should have spent more time on preparation, but you have no intentions to improve, please quit teaching. I can blame whatever I want, but to walk into class not at my best is a disgrace to God's Word and to my church. Make up your mind, however, there is no greater role to play in a local church than to teach!

In another chapter we will discuss the teacher's prayer life and the Spirit of God. Both are extremely important during the week of preparation and the hour of presentation.

We dealt earlier concerning the ***Learning Process***, which helps to assure that learning could take place in your classroom. They could learn, if they would learn, in your class! Below I have included a sample note sheet of how I like to use the process as my guide. Therefore, I can actually organize the lesson to assure the process is covered. Try it at least once to see how it fits you.

3. Organizing Your Lesson

Lesson Title: _____

Text: _____

Step 1

Grab the Attention - State the Facts

Step 2

Define Words/ Terms-Illustrations

Step 3

Personalize the Truth

Step 4

Real Living

The Big 5 _____

_____

_____

4. Remember, You Teach People, Not Lessons

Jesus taught about ability, abstinence, abundant life, access to God, accountability, adultery, adversity, affliction, ambition, angels, anger, anxiety, apostasy, appearance, authority, and that is just some of the *A*'s. In my study Bible, there are mentioned over 400 topics listed in New Testament verses that were teachings and illustrations of Christ, and of course that is not all. Then there are the thirty-seven miracles of Christ, the parables, and more. Real life stuff!

Many of the 400 topics mentioned concerned where people were living. Remember, you teach people who face a multitude of choices and temptations almost daily. Your students have heard that "they ought to" live for Christ. What they need to hear from you is HOW to live for Christ and HOW to avoid sin. That is who you are and what you do. You are their teacher!

Jesus taught people, and all were important for Him and had His full attention. Your students are the same. You must have their attention, and they too must have yours.

When you pray by name and by need, it reminds you that the lesson is not about your quarterly. A quarterly is a help, a guide, a tool, but it does not take center stage. Your lesson today is about the Bible and how it applies to Ted, Zach, Sue, Jeannie, Erica, and Michael. It is about real live people who live in a very wicked world.

Sitting side by side in your classroom, let me describe a scenario. In one chair is Joey, who has never missed a Sunday in his life. In the next chair is Eddie, who for the first time ever is in a Bible class.

Jeannie is the pastor's daughter. Sitting next to her is Erica, who is a drunkard's daughter.

Teddy hates Sunday School, but his parents make him come. Randy sits next to Teddy, and is texting his friend while you teach.

You must have their attention, and they too must have yours.

Sue just lost her Mom to cancer and her Dad is unsaved.

Max and Sarah have two sons on drugs.

That is the real world. Everyone looks great and talks well on Sunday, but Monday- Saturday they are hurting big time.

Teaching is not to exalt myself, but Christ alone who can meet every need.

Jesus taught in parables, which parallel our life styles.

Parable - Lesson

1. The Rich Fool - Foolishness of relying on wealth
2. The Barren Fig Tree - Repent before it is too late
3. The Hidden Treasure - The value of God's kingdom
4. The Good Samaritan - Golden Rule is for all
5. The Good Shepherd - Christ, the only way to God
6. The Wedding Clothes - The necessity of purity
7. The Lost Sheep - Christ's love for sinners
8. The Lost Coin - Christ's love for sinners
9. The Prodigal Son - Christ's love for sinners

10. The Rich man and Lazarus - Riches do not save
11. The Importunate Widow - Persevere in prayer
12. The Talents - Use God's gifts faithfully
13. The Two Sons - Obedience is better than words
14. The Vine and the Branches - Need to abide in Christ
15. The Ten Virgins - Need to be watchful

Obviously, other applications can apply.

Jesus spent His efforts in touching people where they lived. So should we!

There is a prerequisite for the teacher, in that you will need to know the needs of students before planning to meet needs. That is your role as a teacher.

As a teacher of children, I must understand to the best of my ability the children of today, and perhaps more so the children of the last five years. A child's world is vastly different than the one in which you grew up in.

"Until a child is about five years old, he has a hard time distinguishing fantasy from reality. As far as he's concerned, Big Bird is a real friend of his. Barney, the purple dinosaur, can come over and play in the backyard. Animals can talk, and action figures can have real adventures." *Child Sensitive Teaching* by Karyn Henley.

Do you have a clue as to what they watch on TV nowadays? Do you see the examples paraded over the multitude of sitcoms? Sitcoms are one liners- you put me down, then I will put you down; and we will do that for the next thirty minutes, and we will all laugh about it. Do you know the extent of what is being taught in our public schools that is the exact opposite of what you proclaim each Sunday?

*Do you teach **teens**?* Do you understand peer pressure in the current year? Teens don't think the way you think. Their program has been set on a different dial than yours. What does the world look like from their view point? Find out where they are coming from. It will change your selection of content, illustrations, and methods you use.

After years of talking to teens and their teachers, we see clearly that a dull teacher (little enthusiasm, lots of blaming students, almost zero involvement, 95% total lecture each week) often **causes** the dull lesson. Couple that with way too many words, and even you would respond like many teens do. That is not how they learn best.

We must cause them to think, to ponder, to imagine "what if." **Albert Einstein** said, *"Imagination is more important than knowledge."*

*Do you teach **adults**?* Even though many trials, tribulations, and blessings are similar to your own age level, you still do not walk in their shoes. What families are praying for may be vastly different from home to home. Family activities have increased with more social events than ever before, and less time to serve.

As teacher, I cannot ever allow the minor time consumers of life to become more major than my preparation time to teach God's Word. Just be honest with God. Do you or do you not want to be excellent as you handle the Word of God?

5. Choose Less Content, But the Best Content

If your church provided quarterlies especially, you will have before you far more than you can use. The idea is to choose that 40-50-60% of the total which is best for your students.

Now, here comes the hard part. The teacher must get better and better at skimming aside the less significant material provided, without remorse. All lesson notes are not equally important. The teacher's role is to determine the best of all the rest for your class.

"Imagination is more important than knowledge." *Einstein*

In the book *Flight Plan* by Brian Tracy, he says, "One of the most important rules that I have ever learned is this: You are only as free as your well-developed options. . .For example, if you have only one way to accomplish a task and that method does not work, you will be stopped in your tracks. Successful people are continually developing options."

You are not going to look at a prepared quarterly and wonder why they would put such useless notes for you to use. No, it is all good, but there is always a best part of the good. Some material is more "peripheral" than what you can use. It would get you there eventually, but it would take twenty-five minutes to get to where you wanted to go. Then, that leaves you with much less time to say what you know was the most important part.

Be careful with too many points for one lesson. The more you add, the less time you have to clarify any. Actually, the new point will compete with the first two or three for time and the need for further explanation. One major point allows your whole class time to be devoted to making the one point clear! Now, they can all get it!

"It is important to boil it down to a simple sentence statement of purpose. Students complain that teachers are sometimes hard to follow because they never tell you where they are going. Effective teachers have one unifying theme to each teaching session. They do not simply present an outline of information. They present an idea and develop it." – *Creative Bible Teaching* by Richards and Bredfelt.

I would suggest that too much content is a major problem, while running out of lesson notes is not a problem at all. It may force you to review your key thoughts again, which is an excellent "time filler." Review and repetition are always well worth the time spent. Inserting a "what if this happened to you" would help them to "think through" the practicality of your main truth.

My goal should be to "weed out" those non-essential thoughts. I need to get to my one-liner statement or objective in five minutes, then spend all my time saying what I walked into class to say. I do not need to take twenty-five minutes getting to what I really wanted to say, then to realize that I have ten minutes left to say it.

When I get to my point quickly, I now have created more time to say the main thing more than once. When I come to class with less total content than I normally bring, I have more time to illustrate, define words, give a personal illustration, use a marker board, role play a portion, or have a short discussion. Now I can illustrate the truth two or three ways to help all students see it from their perspective!

6. Getting To The Precise Target Quickly

What is that bare-bones knowledge that must be given? This is your goal, your target, the truth that all must see, and the target you cannot miss in this hour. What is that principle for living that could change the student's life? You shoot for it, your illustrations help them to see it, the words you define help to clarify it. In other words, you do not shoot all around it, you shoot directly at it from several different life perspectives. You are covering the bases. You want every student to score! One author compared it to shooting with a shotgun (all over the place) or using a rifle's accuracy.

> *What is that bare-bones knowledge that must be given?*

When you begin to adlib your lesson you will often find yourself bringing up your favorite "axe to grind." There is nothing wrong with spontaneity, but you must avoid the "rabbit trails" so prevalent for teachers. The target cannot jump all over the place, avoiding good accuracy.

Learn to adapt. Most every teacher leans heavily on the "same-o, same-o" style of methods, techniques, and delivery. When you pick up any curriculum it tends to fall into "your style." You will need to practice adapting lesson plans to your major point. Your time slot for teaching will help you to decide what to leave in and what to leave out, as well as how the aim relates to your individual students.

Keep reminding yourself of what your students need. Only you will teach the lesson. Only you have your students. Only you already know the different learning styles of your students. Perhaps all require simple terminology (part of the learning process). Some may learn best visually, by real life illustration, simple discussions which allow for their questions, while some need a hands-on game that relates. Again, all will benefit from almost any visual you use, and all benefit from repetition of your main thought over and over.

Here is a good thought from author David E. Fessenden, in the book *Teaching With All Your Heart.* "Write down a list of the major nouns in the passage, to clarify what is being discussed. List the verbs in the passage to clarify the action taking place. Then list the modifiers (adjectives and adverbs) to make the description in the passage stand out. Do you notice repeated phrases? They are not there by accident; list those as well. Listing the nouns, verbs, modifiers, and repeated phrases can help you catch the vision and intent of the biblical writer."

Good guidance listed above. That is another reason to read books all the time. Someone else will say it better than the last book you read. A little here and a little there is all for your improvement. Become a life-long learner. You and your students will benefit every time.

The teacher must learn to choose less total content in order to thoroughly cover the main point. At best, the more total content you bring to class means that less will be covered thoroughly. If the student does not get it, nothing is going to happen. Now, if you are satisfied with nothing ever happening (something that helps you to verify learning), then do not worry about all of the above. Just teach your lesson again this week and assume they will go home and live that way. I believe you want more out of teaching than that!

Always remember, the accumulation of more and more content is not the highest goal you have. Getting across that one point that could lead to life change is your highest goal. Never forget, this Book can change lives forever and even before you say "class dismissed." However, that will require less total points in order to insure more time to center on more illustrations or discussions or visuals, all on the one-major-key point of all!

Do you get the case I am trying to build? ***Less is actually more*** and so much better for the teacher to prepare for!

7. Mash The Delete Button To Eliminate Time Absorbers

With less total content you are now free to focus on the one major point of it all. Allow me to make a strong suggestion here. In order to improve as a teacher, try to back off on less things that fill your to-do list each week. You may find yourself with 3-4-5 roles to play at your church. That is because you have a very tender heart toward the things of God, and you want your church to reach more. However, because of a multitude of responsibilities you really struggle to come close to a five-hour study period each week on your lesson.

The suggestion is this, give up two or three lesser roles in order to be able to excel in your greater role, that of teacher for God! Listen, I have been in church ministry for over forty years now. Twenty of those years was in a church of 10,000 weekly attendance. I directed the children and teen ministries. Twenty years also in a church of just under 1,000 weekly attendance. I have watched this for years. I have seen the lesson preparation time go from six hours or more to one hour or less. Smaller projects wear you out, and the larger goal gets the pinch and thus suffers. You know it is true.

8. Too Much Is Often Just Too Much

Too much to remember, or too much to apply causes the student to "give up" before he sees reality in his life style. It could be too much of both. Rarely do we apply two or three points into our life in one session. One is usually enough at one time. What is that short, simple, easy to understand point?

To each one the question is: What does this mean in real life?

"Bridging the gap is the term used by Bible expositors to refer to the process by which we make the biblical text relevant to modern living. Good biblical interpretation must ask and answer two questions – what a passage meant to the original audience and what it means to us today. Bridging the gap requires us to perform both activities. This is exactly what is often missing." *Effective Bible Teaching* by **Wilhoit** and **Ryken**.

Give up two or three lesser roles in order to be able to excel in your greater role.

When we use one-point lessons, everything else you add will support, prove, illustrate, repeat, and make it easier to understand and retain.

One point lessons help me to eliminate rabbit trails and detours! Why bring up multiple needs, unless the goal is to thoroughly teach each, and make application to each?

So, why am I teaching this lesson anyway? What would be the ideal outcome? What is the ultimate destination, the finish line, the take it home truth? Am I bringing too much? By the time I hit point 5, have they forgotten 1-2-3-4?

If content is major, the time to say the main thing more than once becomes minor. If your time slips away without time to say your main thought 10-12 times during the lesson, then do no expect it to hit home or even last as long as they get home.

If usually the last point is what stays better in the mind of your student, then why not make the last point the whole point throughout the hour? The repetition from beginning to end of the one-main-major-essential-priority point cannot possibly be forgotten.

Repetition is what makes it stick! But, a heavy dose of content, assures less time for repetition. Now with a one-point lesson here is what happens:

1. It is the bottom line "take-home and remember" point of all points.

2. Now, I can illustrate the same one-point 3-4 times, to better touch each student whose lives are within different backgrounds.

3. The repetition fixes that one-key-principle in the mind of each.

4. Every illustration or discussion or role-play or personal testimony will enhance understanding.

5. Your students can now write down the one-point. They can see it, say it, read it maybe 10-12 times before your class ends.

6. The retention value is assured over and over. When there is more to be remembered, it usually winds up with less remembered.

In the well-written book *Talk Like Jesus* by **Lynn Wilford Scarborough**, *"Word pictures create a visual with words that help explain, frame or illustrate a point. They are short memorable phrases that make the complex easy to understand."*

9. You Have A Higher Mandate When You Teach!

If teaching God's Word is the biggest role you have at church, then, stop some other roles so that teaching may flourish. Why would I give less and less to teaching, because more and more little things are consuming my time? Why would I do that? Let the "pew sitters" do the smaller things. Set your goal higher than ever before. Put into practice good tools to aid you and to help you!

Dale Burke reminds us to think big: "First you want to focus on goals that, if accomplished, will make a significant difference in the growth or quality of the ministry. Many leaders devote most of their energy toward goals that are heavy on maintenance and light on mission."

Wow! Did he ever hit the mark! Guess what ministry you have that is heavy on mission? He also reminds us, "Keep your dreams more exciting than your memories. When your memories are more exciting than your dreams, you've begun to die." *Less Is More Leadership*

10. Master Your Lesson (A Key To Communication)!

The reason you want to master your lesson:

1. It will allow you the freedom from so many notes.
2. The amount of eye-contact from your students is very brief, as you can always scan in three seconds what comes next.
3. It allows you more eye contact to notice the student's facial expressions. Their expressions will tell you quickly "how you're doing" in clarifying the truth.

4. It forces you to be in control of your notes, rather than many pages of notes in control of you.

5. You will be better open to response from students, as you see their expressions.

6. Without having to return to your notes to see what comes next, a quick glance eliminates the "dead time" when attention has opportunity to fly away.

7. As teacher, you can be more spontaneous and alert to the Spirit of God and His inner urges that keep you on the main track.

If my notes are actually like a "security blanket" to me, it may mean I need to put a little more into my week of preparation.

For example, if my illustration concerns a home mailbox, or fishing, or an illustration from children, then why can I not study this well enough at home so I can simply put in my notes the word *mailbox* or *fishing*. Why should I need to run back to my notes, find where I left off, see enough of what comes next, then finally put my eyes back on my students? Why cannot I know and have practiced exactly what I need to say? In most cases, it is because I have spent too little time in preparation.

So, I must go back to my notes (lose eye-contact), reread a portion of what comes next (dead time) to remember what to say. It only takes those few seconds for students to lose focus and to refocus their eyes and minds on other things. Now, you will have to regain their attention again. Let that happen 15-20 times during your lesson and you will find it tough to keep their thoughts on track to the end.

The better approach and more fulfilling class is when you are a "Ready-Freddy" teacher. If your notes blew out the window, it would be alright, because you have learned to ***master the lesson!***

11. Clarifying God's Truth Leads To Changing Lives!

I have had the privilege for thirty-five years to cross this country trying to train church teachers in practical principles of teaching. It is amazing to me that we can go for years and years "assuming" that our teachers are pretty good at this thing we call communication. Yet, most leaders have never heard their teachers actually teach. "Well, she's a wonderful person, with a great family." So, with that we have somehow concluded that the same person has no need of improvement in the area of communicating a lesson.

a. We Assume Too Much, Way Too Much

For all these years I have come to an unavoidable conclusion that most leaders have been "assuming way too much" for a long time. When teaching the Bible is such a high priority in our churches, yet the training of those same teachers is totally absent, something is missing. I am in some very large churches which have never had training in thirty years. It is always on the back burner, always gets delayed, and always planned for "someday."

Add to who you are and what you do.

The purpose of this book is to add to a growing group of helps available. The quotes we use here are from books worth buying and reading. You must improve yourself, not only from books and ideas of others but from your own experiences and evaluation. Add to who you are and what you do!

b. What Is A "Win" For You?

Most companies keep some kind of scoreboard. Perhaps our scoreboard should be as large and as up-to-date as what we see in the basketball game at the Coliseum downtown. There you have no doubt at all of who is winning, the score, the time to the hundredth of a second, and which quarter of the game we are in.

If scoring runs wins a baseball game or touchdowns win in football, what would be a first quarter win in your class next week? Half way through, could you conclude that you are winning or losing? Are you right on target, behind, or way behind? Can you look at your progress on any day of the week, and see if you feel good about your lesson preparation or do you need to speed it up?

Would you look at yourself and what you are spending your time on as a $100 an hour worker, or a $10 an hour worker? In other words, you should be planning the lesson as if you are the $100 an hour planner. Thus, are you putting your time on the "meat" of the lesson? That means how much time is on the one-line objective? Whatever aids or helps you use to prepare your lesson, there will be lots of ideas that are *peripheral*. They will get you there, but it will take most of your time just to get to where you wanted to go. Clarifying your goal will settle that from the beginning.

c. "Words without actions are the assassins of dreams."

This quote is from *An Enemy Called Average*, by **John L. Mason.** Time spent on less productive projects is the assassin of your dreams and goals for that which is your responsibility. The secret of any success we may have is based upon our best use of what we are best gifted for. Spend more time developing and enhancing the gifts and the abilities you have than in the areas of which you are not so gifted.

Getting it done is determined by your weekly agenda planned for lesson preparation. The suggested time slots I have earlier for a week of preparation are all subject to your change and your weekly schedule. The idea is to rework the plan suggested to a workable plan for you. But, if you learn to use the 80/20 plan, as a multitude of the books in the bookstore refer to, great production could take place. Give 80% of your effort to the top 20% of lesson ideas you select as most important. Get to the point quickly and stay there throughout your week, working and improving those key thoughts and ideas.

Clarification involves all of these areas to consider. **Dedicate yourself** to becoming absolutely excellent in what you do. Management of your time enables you to increase the value of your contribution.

Time Power by **Brian Tracy** says, "Everything you accomplish depends on your ability to use your time to its best advantage. You can only increase your quality and quantity of your results by increasing your ability to use your time effectively."

Dedicate yourself to becoming absolutely excellent in what you do.

Communicating thoroughly is your role, your duty, and your best move! What really matters? What is really worth the time and effort? That is why your main objective will lead only to that which gets it across clearly. "The single biggest problem in communication is the illusion that it has taken place," **George Benard Shaw**. Seek to be specific with what your major thought is.

For ten years I worked at Pratt-Whitney Aircraft in research and development for the early space program from Canaveral. The "wins" there in research for later production would amount to millions for the company and for NASA. The measurements and the quality control demanded the work force be absolutely knowledgeable, without any reservation, as to the target. At times we could hold in one hand a part that cost over $100,000; and you could ruin it in three seconds. The goal to be reached would demand perfection to the entire operation. The company's reputation, the crewmen aboard, and so much more demanded that every piece of work had a clear clarification attached. There were no unanswered questions.

d. Why Can't Our Bible Lessons Be So Clear?

Why can my students not understand without any doubts whatsoever? Why cannot the teachers in my church "so clarify what God has to say that the student could not possibly miss it"? Could you so prepare that you could identify your lesson as a "win"?

"Effective teachers have learned to travel slowly. They know that they often teach more by teaching less. . . Instead it involves acknowledging that a stream of unrelated or marginally related ideas soon wearies a listener. Good teachers know what is important and make the important ideas clear to their students." *Effective Bible Teaching* by **Jim Wilhoit and Leland Ryken.**

Clarity of the words and terms cannot be taken for granted because your students have been around Bible classes long enough that they have no need of definitions or illustrations anymore. All you have to do is ask for definitions of words or terms and you will find out quickly that you need clarification.

Clarity of words and terms cannot be taken for granted.

A nod of the head does not necessarily mean that the student knows what you know. They have been nodding their head since a four-year-old child. We have taught them to do that. Perhaps you need to un-teach yourself some techniques you still use that tell you virtually nothing.

Time has to be allowed to clearly and thoroughly help them to see your main thought. Clarity continues into your illustration, your visuals, your stories, and all the methods and techniques you use.

So, whether students decide to obey God or not in their own choices, you cannot control their decisions or make them decide what choice you would make. *The part you can control is the clarity you give to the lesson.* Your role is to so teach that the student could not possibly miss what God has to say. Keep this word before you during the week of preparation – *CLARIFY!*

12. Including All Students In Ways They Each Learn Best!

People learn best in different ways. They also prefer one or more techniques over other forms of communication styles used on them. Some will forget the key thought without a visual reminder. Others need to write it down, while some would learn better if allowed to ask questions. Reading a passage along with the speaker would help everyone to see it, say it, and hear it.

The goal then is not necessarily just to limit communication to my personal style of speaking but to try to touch as many learning styles as possible. Illustrations and storytelling are two techniques that help every learner. Remember, unlike your socks, one size does not fit all. Think through the multi-sensory methods that Jesus used: the parables (an earthly story, fully understood by all, with a heavenly meaning). Jesus used what was appropriate for the person and the situation.

Jesus used whatever was around Him that people could see. Remember the teachings of a corn of wheat, water, vines-branches, animals, clay, wine, boats, fish, and fishermen. Then there are the parables, picturing real life in a multitude of real life situations.

The Tabernacle was a visual image of how to worship God in the Old Testament. The cross immediately pictures the grace of God. As you sing songs, the visual images race through your mind. The Lord's Supper asks us to remember the death, burial, and resurrection. It is an inward look, and upward look, and a backward look.

Baptism is a picture that identifies us with our Savior. Sitting in a classroom back in 1972, I noticed a simple visual hand movement that illustrated the picture of baptism. With the professor's hand he illustrated what the picture meant. He first held his hand vertical to indicate the death of Christ on the cross, then dropped his hand to horizontal to picture death (as with Christ in an earthy grave and us in a watery grave), then raised his hand again to vertical to picture the resurrection and to walk in newness of life. Immediately, I said to myself, that is a good way to help children understand the purpose of baptism.

Baptism is our identification that we have died to a life of sin, I am buried with Christ, and I too rise to walk in newness of life. I say to the world that I am a Christian, a follower of Christ!

My salvation came upon my initial believing and receiving of the Son of God (John 3:18). Baptism then became my personal testimony of what

Christ did for me when I believed. Baptism is both an act of our obedience to God's command and a picture to the world that I identify with Christ. My submission to baptism pictured what had already taken place. You cannot take a physical substance, water, and produce a spiritual result. It is a picture, an identification.

Since that first baptism tract, with this picture, I have now seen ten- a total of ten baptism tracts with this identical simple drawing in it. Almost all have the original drawing with a flair pen that I did thirty-nine years ago. That does not bother me; it just shows the power of a simple visual.

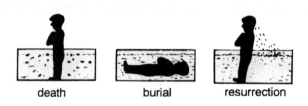

death   burial   resurrection

I have had many missionaries return to say, "Bro. Abb, when we use that tract it really helps people to understand. You can use all the verses and comment on the tract, but when they come to that visual, you can 'see it in their eyes,' they get it! Most often their comment is 'Oh, I see now!'" Jesus taught that way all the time!

A visual does not change the message of Scripture, it enhances it and clarifies it.

God gave us the senses for use, daily use, hourly use, and most people in the world have all their senses intact.

In his book *The Power Of Mulit-Sensory Preaching and Teaching* by **Rick Blackwood**, he reminds us "God gave us this amazing universe; he communicates the universe through sound, vision, feel, smell, and taste; and he gave us the five corresponding senses to perceive it."

So, what was the purpose in this long parenthesis about visual learning? I wish to make a strong reminder that many students worldwide are visual-dominant learners. It is their best and easiest way to understand and to retain. Teachers who simply "talk all the time" can easily ignore and certainly bore several of their students. Try not to ignore the preferred method of learning for any and all of your students.

Again, *Rick Blackwood* gives us a good illustration: "In research conducted by Nater and Rollins, they found an alarming statistic about learning preferences. They looked at 1,500 adults who had dropped out of school in the eighth grade and found that 99.60 percent of them were sensing-dominant learners. In other words, they were visual and interactive learners."

> *You will have students who differ in their best way to learn.*

The idea here is simple. You too will have students who differ in their best way to learn. Try not to leave anyone out! The illustration above shows us that these type learners were taught by teachers who were heavy on words and light on visuals.

13. Focus Keeps You On Target!

You need focus when you teach a lesson that could possibly change the lives of students!

1. The Teacher Must Choose To Focus.

You can always keep adding to, but never subtracting from a multitude of good comments. Each add-on comments will suck-up more time from your critical time of finishing while leaving less time for the "Big Five."

A single minded determination, such as your very clear *one-line objective* for your lesson is a must. Would it not be a wonderful lesson if you so focused on one single thought? Then, you had time to illustrate the point two or three ways, discuss it, go through a series of thought-provoking questions, give a personal illustration, define terms, and to personalize that truth to where the student could not possibly miss it. Everything was focused on the one truth. The goal would truly strike home!

H. Dale Burke, in *Less is More Leadership* makes this great statement, "Specialization does not mean you are doing less; in fact, you are doing more. But you are doing more of your best stuff, instead of just stuff." In light of a Sunday school lesson, you focus on giving your best comments, methods and techniques to that one overriding truth, not general suggestions covering several areas of life. Focus!

When you take the time to focus on the one-main-key-truth, you begin to see many other notes as peripheral, having little to do with the goal of your lesson.

We must value our time. It is all we have. Someone said, "Greatness lies in the right use of strength." Our strength is found in our focus on that one-major-truth of God for this week.

When we focus on those high-dividend (life changing) projects, we see good things happen. Getting out of the "generalities" and into the "specifics" is what students need. Tell me *How* please, someone please show me *How!* Focus allows you to drive the point home, so that the student could not possibly miss it.

> *Our strength is found in our focus.*

Whatever your major goal for this lesson, it deserves your greatest effort and teaching skills. Time and effort given to non-critical areas need to decrease as soon as possible. You must make those decisions during your week of preparation, to avoid rabbit trails, non-focused questions, and following all the additional thoughts that cross your mind while teaching. We are all capable of adding thoughts we had no idea of giving. Losing focus robs us of focus.

In this week's lesson, what will bring the highest returns? Then, 80% of your thinking and planning should go into that which bears fruit!

Dr. Howard Hendricks said, "If anything has kept me on track all these years, it is being skewered to this principle of central focus. There are many things I can do, but I have to narrow it down to the one thing I must do. The secret of concentration is elimination."

As teacher, you must focus on evaluating whether the lesson plan will get you to the final step. The passion or drive inside is fed by the mission of your lesson objective.

In teaching, often eliminating is our answer. When we focus on less, it allows concentration on that which will keep you on the proper track. We know that. That is not revolutionary. Focus fixes the steps that will lead exactly to the truth.

Whatever your focus becomes your main thought. It becomes your whole mission for that hour.

"The mission is what you exist for, and everything is secondary to the mission. . .The vision has to be clear. It has to be straight forward. It has to be understandable. But above all, it has to be achievable, and it has to be something that will cause people to believe so that they will want to follow you and not just *have* to follow you." – Secretary of State, **Colin L. Powell**, 2003 "Leadership Lecture."

Get to it quickly, stay there, clarify, and illustrate the truth in real everyday life. It is all part of your week of preparation!

A Review Of Key Thoughts:

1. Just in your thoughts, compare the suggested time schedule per week to study, with what you have going. How could you improve, instead of waiting so late in the week to get started? _____

_____

_____

2. Your students have heard for years that "they ought to" live for Christ. What they need to hear from you is _____ to live and _____ to avoid.

3. From memory, describe how each of your students are different from others, especially in learning styles. _____

_____

_____

4. You are an *adult* teacher. The lesson is overcoming temptation. From your memory, name two couples who should have a great personal testimony to share with the class on temptation and the victory God gave.

(1) _____ (2) _____

5. For next week's lesson, what would be your "one-liner" objective, or purpose for teaching?_____

_____

6. Define to yourself what it means to "master your lesson." _____

_____

_____

Chapter FIVE

The Spirit Of God In It All! / The Prayer Life Of The Teacher

Chapter Five brings us to consider two essential qualities in our week of preparation and our hour of presentation: (1) The Spirit of God In Your Teaching! (2) The Prayer Life of the Teacher!

What does it mean to give the Spirit of God liberty to break into your lesson? How can you allow Him to close-out your lesson?

The Spirit of God In Your Teaching

1. Go To Him First! Ask Him To Help You!

2. The Spirit Of God Is The Teacher Of All Teachers!

3. He Is Ready, Able, And Waiting To Help You!

4. Listen To Him As You Choose Your Content!

5. Give Him Liberty In Your Presentation Time!

6. Allow Him To Close Out Your Class!

The Prayer Life Of The Teacher!

1. You Must Pray To Have Your Prayers Answered

2. Do Not Wait Until You Are Finished To Start Praying

3. Pray Specifically: By Name, By Need

4. Pray For Wisdom- Knowledge- Understanding

V. The Spirit Of God In Your Teaching The Prayer Life Of The Teacher

1. Go To Him First! Ask Him To Help You!

The Holy Spirit is the One who produces godlike character in each person who believes.

"The Spirit of Truth. John 14:47; 15:26; 16:13; I John 5:6. As God is Love, so the Spirit is Truth. He possesses, reveals, confesses, leads into, testifies to, and defends the truth. He is opposed to the 'spirit of error' (I John 4:6)." ***The Great Doctrines Of The Bible,*** by William Evans.

Why would I lessen the great value of the Spirit of God in my area of teaching by avoiding His presence in my week of preparation and continuing to act as though His presence is not necessary during my presentation? That is one big question, although we would like to assume it never happens to us. We surely would not do that intentionally, but just may do exactly that unintentionally.

As we are to practice the presence of the Spirit of God daily in our Christian walk, He must be welcome in both our preparation and presentation. It is almost unbelievable that we can be so shallow as to "forget" how significant the Spirit of God is in us daily and in the convicting and transforming power He has in our students. Never, never go it alone.

We know He is always there because of His indwelling in every Christian, yet *practically* it could be as He is not present in our classroom. That is because of our shallow practicing of His presence.

The Spirit of God is sent from the Father and the Son. He represents them, as we would think of an executive, doing exactly what Jesus would do if He walked this earth again and held our hand step by step. I must not ignore or forget Him.

We must be careful in our day and time not to go to the extreme of avoiding His work because of the TV programs which seem to make more of the Spirit's work than of the Father and the Son. Perhaps we should go back to our book on doctrine where we were first aided to understand the great doctrines of God, Jesus Christ, Holy Spirit, Man, Salvation, Church, Scriptures, Angels, Satan, and Last Things. It was very clear there as they pointed us to the Scriptures which testified of the truthful workings of each.

Allow the Spirit of God into your week of lesson preparation. Walk into your classroom with more assurance of God's choice of content than ever before. Feel His presence in a greater way than ever before!

2. The Spirit Of God Is The Teacher Of All Teachers

"But the anointing which ye have received of him abideth in you, and ye need not that any man teach you: but as the same anointing teacheth you of all things, and is truth, and is no lie, and even as it hath taught you, ye shall abide in him." I John 2:27

You have the privilege and the right to ask for knowledge and teaching for yourself. A prepared curriculum is not bad, it is a help, a guide, a tool, or an aid. It becomes an incorrect use when I put my trust in it alone. This can easily occur when my week of preparation has been put off and off until the week is now the busy weekend before the Lord's Day.

Now, I grab for the first thing that looks like some kind of outline that can get me through another week. With a few prepared notes (prepared by someone else) I can literally "adlib" my way through, while calling it a Bible class. Shame on me! May God forgive me!

It is simply not enough to rely on human teachers or helpers, without allowing the time needed for the Spirit of God to teach you.

If you will read I Corinthians 2:9-14 it reminds you that some great truths are spiritually discerned. Discernment means to have keen perception or judgment; insight; to recognize as different. To perceive or recognize; to make out clearly is discernment.

"But the Comforter, which is the Holy Ghost, whom the Father will send in my name, he shall teach you all things, and bring all things to your remembrance, whatsoever I have said unto you." John 14:26

The Spirit of God will interpret the Scriptures for you to teach a clear understanding to your students (I Cor. 2:9-14).

Start early in the week. Get all the help you can, as early as you can, and continue this thrust throughout your week of preparation and take off presentation!

3. He Is Ready, Able, And Waiting To Help You!

Could the Holy Spirit *"squeeze"* into your preparation and into your presentation? You desperately need Him! He is ready when you are. When you read the new passage for the first time, He is ready, standing by to teach you!

Seek His power to hover over your study. He is God! Omnipotent – Luke 1:35, Omniscient – I Corinthians 2:10-11; Omnipresent – Psalm 139:1-13.

Among your believing students He regenerates, indwells, anoints, baptizes, guides, empowers, sanctifies, bears witness, comforts, gives joy, gives discernment, bears fruit, gives gifts, and much more.

4. Listen To Him As You Choose Your Content

If you use a printed curriculum, you already know that you could not use it all anyway, and must pick and choose. Ask the Spirit of God to help you choose the best from all the rest. He knows your students, all of them. He knows their needs, their spiritual "temperature," their fears, and their need for this lesson.

He will help you go beyond generalities to the specifics. Then He will remind you where the truth fits in the lives of your individual students. You do not always know that, but He does, as we saw earlier.

The Spirit of God gives discernment as you teach:
"But God hath revealed them unto us by his Spirit: for the Spirit searcheth all things, yea, the deep things of God. For what man knoweth the things of a man, save the spirit of man which is in him? Even so the things of God knoweth no man, but the Spirit of God. Now we have received, not the spirit of the world, but the spirit which is of God; that we might know the things that are freely given to us of God." I Corinthians 2:10-12

The Spirit of God reproves us of sin (and unbelief). *"And when he (Comforter/ Spirit) is come, he will reprove the world of sin, and of righteousness and of judgment." (parentheses added) John 16:8*

You cannot do that, but He can! Recognize that. When you provide "pauses" along the way you allow for the truth to be witnessed to by the Spirit of God. Sometimes, one pause by you will be worth more to the student than thirty more words! It is like the *"Selahs"* God gives in His Word.

He reveals to you and your students God's truth: *"Howbeit when he, the Spirit of truth is come, he will guide you into all truth: for he shall not speak of himself; but whatsoever he shall hear, that shall he speak: and he will shew you things to come." John 16:13*

You must have an **emptiness of self** in order to be ready for God's filling, and you need to pray for His filling to empower your teaching. The filling of God's Spirit is an often gift to you, if you are right for the filling. Empty of self every day and the filling of God every day is the goal, and nothing less! As Christians, we already know that, but within your own heart, when was the last time that actually happened?

Do you remember the times you drove to church with that feeling of unpreparedness and the feeling that you are all on your own? It is a most empty feeling (*I confess*), and it should be.

Just as Christ reminded His disciples to take full advantage of their God who has all power (Luke 12:1-12) and to trust Him at all times: *"For the Holy Ghost shall teach you in the same hour what ye ought to say,"* as we see in verse 12.

In like manner the Holy Spirit's work can help you to know what to say and how to say it, as pertaining to your lesson. In Deuteronomy 6:7 God speaks of teaching the children **"diligently."** That is still the best method of teaching.

"Diligently" is still defined as "persevering and careful in work; hardworking, done with careful, steady effort; painstaking." Preparing lessons and teaching need not be an ordeal to suffer each week, but "painstaking" can be your level of dedication to the Savior, to the Word, and to His calling upon you!

Allowing the Spirit of God to choose your content is a wonderful way to surrender the next lesson to Him. Read a portion, think it through in light of real names in your class and listen for that "still, small voice." There will be perhaps 40-50% of all that content that will relate almost immediately.

Take what the Holy Spirit of God impresses you with and skim the other aside, without remorse. This works the best early in the week, as we suggested in *Lesson Preparation*. Go to Him first and early in the week.

5. Give Him Liberty In Your Presentation Time

We often hear our pastor praying for the "liberty" of a visiting speaker to have as he preaches in our church. This is not only a prayer for the liberty of the Spirit to have control of the preacher during the message, but for the Spirit to have liberty within all of us who hear the message.

In other words, "Holy Spirit of God, have your way in our heart and do whatever you wish in me." You are expressing yourself to the Lord to touch you however He wills!

The way you give the Spirit of God liberty is to start early and listen for the thoughts He puts in your mind. Then, watch for occasions during your week when a real-life illustration ties into your lesson. It is the Spirit trying to impress you. Keep a small note card handy to record your thoughts immediately. The more you bring up the names of students, the more you are allowing the Spirit liberty to show you what should be your emphasis for Joe and Sue and Danny, or the Riddle family. Add that thought to your growing thoughts for your students!

The Spirit of God has lived with the student all week long (the saved student). He has gone where they have gone. He knows what they fed into their mind this week (TV, magazines, conversations, and some gossip). When you pray specifically with real names, He will enlighten you of their needs and impress one or more verses in the passage. That is where you will need to spend your time!

The Spirit's insight impressed upon you will cause you to add into your notes a role play for some, an illustration for all, a Bible illustration that matches the situation, or occasionally a personal illustration that shows the consequences, whether good or bad. That is who He is and that is what He does!

Learn to use the pause as you teach. The pause in your talking allows the Spirit of God to work on the hearts of students about what you just said. Bring two or three of your key one-liner statements for such a time as a pause. In Scripture, it is like the "Selah" you see in the Old Testament.

Learn to pause. It is dialogue, not a monologue. The pause gives your people a chance to consider what you have just said. It gives their minds a needed break. The best time to do this is when you are saying something especially significant. John Maxwell said, "Everybody communicates, few connect."

Another aid to giving liberty is the preparation time you gave this week. A well prepared teacher has liberty. This means that you know your lesson so well (mastery), that you cannot wait to begin! Now, with one half page of "reminder" words you are at liberty from many pages of notes. You are at liberty to look your students in the eye and use your full line of emotions, feelings, expressions, and gestures from your face to your whole body. Now, you are free to really communicate. Prepare yourself well, and ask God for liberty in the classroom!

6. Allow Him To Close Out Your Class

In chapter three we touched on the last 5 minutes of class time and how to spend that conclusion of your lesson. Let me note again two lines of that chapter: *"We all know that when a spiritual change takes place it all comes down to **just me and just God.** But, without my time to respond to Him it is only another reminder that 'I ought to,' someday."*

I believe, after forty years of dealing with teachers, this is the biggest error in teaching. Why did I teach that lesson anyway? Was it for more knowledge of God's Word? Certainly! But is there something even greater than knowing more and more about the Bible? Yes, there is! It is life-change that leads me not just to stack this lesson on top of several thousand others, but to receive it, believe it, and live it! That is greater and that is pleasing to God.

*"And why call ye me, Lord, Lord, and **do not** the things which I say?"* Luke 6:46
*"Therefore to him that knoweth to do good and **doeth it not,** to him it is sin."* James 4:17
*"If ye **continue in my word,** then are ye my disciples indeed."* John 8:31
*"Ye are my friends, if ye **do** whatsoever I command you."* John 15:14

The part that is often missing in our lesson is the time allotted to say **"Yes, Lord!"** Transformation from knowing to living in obedience comes when I respond back to God about what He just taught me. Here is where the Spirit of God urges and compels the believer to be a "doer of the Word, and not a hearer only." But, the teacher is in the position to allow the Spirit of God time to draw the student to obedience. There has to be that response time.

Yet, in our church, pastor would never miss such an opportunity (*the invitation*), while in Sunday school class we rarely, if ever, allow time for a response. Thus, we say "nice lesson" to our teacher, but it never seems to change me.

What is the solution? The solution is to change my former way of ending the class. Allow that last 4-5 minute time a quiet response time back to God. You make the judgment call as to each week, or on a particular lesson.

How can we walk away feeling good about our teaching, yet we have not actually seen students change in the last 10-20 years? We see change take place in the church service, but never in our classroom. Every change comes down to **"just me and just God."** When such a time is not allowed, the devil will see to it that the truth fades quickly away.

Take another look at the numerous verses and passages that teach us about the Spirit of God and how He helps us:

Luke 12:12 "For the Holy Ghost shall teach you in the same hour what ye ought to say." In the moment you need His help, He is there. This verse may be applied in several ways. As in this context it was to remind his witnesses that the Holy Ghost will give them what they need when they needed it. Hey, that is you, right in the middle of your lesson!

This truth goes for a teacher of God's Word too, both in your week of preparation and your hour of presentation. However, that does not allow me to head to class unprepared and expect Him to move my mouth with every word to say. The lack of preparation will find you muttering, sputtering, and adlibbing your way the whole class hour. The Spirit of God will enhance your words that you have *prepared and prayed over all week!*

We looked at this before, but here we need to be reminded again:
In John 14:26 the Lord's promise to you is this: ***"But the Comforter, which is the Holy Ghost, whom the Father will send in my name, he shall teach you all things, and bring all things to your remembrance, whatsoever I have said unto you."***

The Comforter will be there to give you that quick reminder, to push the emotion and feeling out of your voice as you teach. He will cause your eyes to fall upon one student after another and will also *"bring to your remembrance"* an illustration or a way to say it that gets their attention. It may not have been in your notes, but just the small extra comment or special look or expression is what clarified the truth to the student.

We must be so empty of self, so filled with the Spirit that we can be sensitive to what the Spirit is saying to us. We can differentiate His urges between our adlibbing or our rabbit trails we are prone to get on. That is a wonderful way to teach.

To me, it is like the Holy Spirit is calling the signals, while I am the pitcher. His voice is in my ear before every pitch. When I hear "Strike!" it energizes me to throw another strike for the Lord! If I hear "Ball," I need to elaborate more, or add a slower (change-up) ball, or get back on target. Sounds silly, but it might help those of us familiar to strikes, balls, outs, and the occasional perfect game.

In the game of baseball, I pitched for a long time. I know that control was not an automatic. It did not just come because I was pitching today. It came because from an eight-year-old boy, I practiced control more than all my sliders, fast balls, curves, ins 'n outs, and change-ups. My Dad was my first "catcher" in our back yard. He knew something that I did not know then – that control will make or break you. He also knew that it only comes after long-time practices. As I grew older, he would suffer the pains of my fast ball. But suffer he did. It is wonderful to remember those days!

In high school ball I could throw some nice curves, but if they never crossed the home plate it did not matter. In college I could throw some at 90 miles an hour, but if they had no control, it did not matter. As you watch the better pitchers today, you will be impressed by their control. It is because they have practiced for years and years. Now they can throw their fast balls and curves with control. That is what is impressive and that is what wins!

In teaching, you want to win every time you "take the field!" The wonderful Spirit of God is there to help you with your control!

For the sake of Christ, take some time alone to think through these few thoughts on the working of the Spirit of God in your week of preparation and your hour of presentation. Do you start early enough to allow Him time? Do you feel like you can make it on your own? Is the filling of the Spirit of God on your mind each day, or only a scant few times within the year? Meditate on Him and pray that the Lord God will make these things so in your life, then, transferred to your classroom!

The Prayer Life Of The Teacher!

1. You Must Pray To Have Your Prayers Answered

Sometimes we tend to leave out the basic principle, and load up on all the other peripheral things. They are often good too, it is just that there is often a better choice in where to spend my time. Then, someone brings us back to the basics with a simple thought that seems to wrap it all up.

We can study a whole course on prayer, a series of 13 lessons on prayer, read a 400 page book on prayer, learn things such as to whom do we pray, for what do we pray, when do we pray, for how long do we pray, times to pray, attitudes of prayer, positions of prayer, and study every key verse of prayer in our Bible.

Yet, with all the above – **never pray.** So, to start us off, remember prayer is just that – it is praying to your great God, in the name of His blessed Son.

"Giving thanks always for all things unto God and the Father, in the name of our Lord Jesus Christ." Ephesians 5:20

Look at some key words and the order:
"Giving" – Giving what? – *"Giving thanks"* – How often? – *"Always"* – For what? – *"For all things"* – Unto whom? – *"Unto God"* – What else? – *"In the name..."*

Just like other requests we wish for God to answer, this example of "Giving thanks" shows us the pattern for all our prayers – He says to *give it, give it, give it!* It begins there, and has wonderful results.

So, when and how often do you pray about next week's class time? You have several significant areas to address in your prayers: (1) That the Spirit of God will begin early in the week to give you wisdom (2) That He would impress you as to the content you choose and that which you discard (3) To help you as you pray by student name and need (4) To ask Him to teach you the lesson in real life before Sunday (5) To help you to organize and master the lesson and touch the hearts of your students (6) To enlarge your passion for teaching and your compassion for people.

You will find many other reasons to pray during the week. *The key is to pray.* If you could list the times you actually pray during the week on one-hand of fingers, you probably have an inadequate prayer life as a teacher.

2. Do Not Wait Until You Are Finished To Start Praying

You must go to God early, often, and with a great compassion for those names and faces you will see on Sunday. This demands more than the shallowness of "Lord, bless my class next week." No names, no specifics, just "bless 'em all dear Lord." You cannot afford to be so lax in your prayer life. You are praying on their behalf, and they desperately need it. Beyond that, you desperately need it.

I have been there, and it is an awful feeling to head to church and your class and it is almost like the first time I remembered to pray. Oh, I did pray, but it was shallow and so specific-less, I wonder if God even listened. I had no idea what this lesson would mean to Joe and Stan, to Jean and Charlotte, or the other ten teens in my class. The feeling is bad, and it should be so bad that I would never want to prepare like that again.

The good news is that it does not have to happen, ever! After working out your own time frame for your week of preparation, determining to stay on track each week, *make sure your prayer time is on the list.*

3. Pray Specifically: By Name, By Need

We have already mentioned enough reminders of praying by name and need for your students. Let me give you note of a helpful booklet:

The Discipleship Roll Book

Section 1 This section helps to organize any prospects met for your class. Keep track of good prospects. Do not lose these names and addresses.

Section 2 A very easy way to track your class attendance. It is always with you, with enough space for the whole year, plus new students throughout the year.

Section 3 One of the best sections is where your discipleship of students will record all the details you need on each student. A great help in praying and helping you to recognize areas of life, specifically on each student, and room for a picture.

Section 4 The Prayer and Praise Diary follows to keep your prayer life on track. Record here what you are praying about with this student. By name, by need, and a place to list your praises when God answers them one by one.

Section 5 The very end includes block calendars for the whole year, to make your plans for visiting students, discipleship, or activities.

This booklet is compact, up-to-date, and ready for your use year round! Find these in our Product Catalog from Master Ministries (MASTERCLUBS. ORG).

4. Pray For Wisdom – Knowledge – Understanding

Our Lord makes it so clear we cannot miss it and so clear that we can attain what He offers.

"So that thou incline thine ear unto wisdom, and apply thine heart to understanding. Yea, if thou criest after knowledge, and liftest up thy voice for understanding. For the Lord giveth wisdom: out of his mouth cometh knowledge and understanding." Proverbs 2:2-3,6

You need all three, and you need them from the very start of your preparation week.

The first four chapters of Proverbs are worth reading multiple times, pausing to think it through and in your mind apply it to your role of teaching and how to deal with people (students).

Some short quick thoughts:

a. Go After It – It Is Available
Wisdom in Proverbs is *"to be wise"* or to *"act wisely;" "apply thine heart;" "criest after knowledge;" "seeketh her;" "searcheth for her;" "keep sound wisdom and discretion;" "get wisdom;" "get understanding;" "forget*

it not;" "exalt her." The use of the feminine noun here of "her" refers to wisdom. Search for her, get her, find her; that is wisdom. Sounds like God wants us to pursue this great truth! Therefore, it must be attainable.

Proverbs reminds us of the value in getting and keeping wisdom and knowledge and understanding!

b. Trust God For It

"Trust in the Lord with all thine heart; and lean not unto thine own understanding. In all thy ways acknowledge him, and he shall direct thy paths." Proverbs 3:5,6

We have known that verse from childhood, at least the words we could quote. One of the most beautiful thoughts from God for a teacher in our week of preparation and our hour of presentation! There is great benefit in having wisdom from God!

God demonstrated through Solomon the wisdom that He could give to a man. In I Kings 4:29 we read, *"And God gave Solomon wisdom and understanding exceeding much, and largeness of heart, even as the sand that is on the sea shore."* In verse 31, *"For he was wiser than all men. . . and his fame was in all nations."* In verse 32, *"And he spake three thousand proverbs: and his songs were a thousand and five."* Biblical wisdom comes from God, reflects God, and is for your use in whatever you do to glorify Him!

Moral wisdom is not drawn from sinful men, but from our sinless Lord. That is why Proverbs 3:5 and 6 reminds us to *realize* this, *surrender* to and *trust* in God's wisdom, ***"and he shall direct thy paths."***

This book will teach you to be a wise teacher. This wisdom is not just a theory, but a practice. The practice of this truth makes it applicable and practical as you communicate to students. *Do not leave home without the wisdom of God!*

It is interesting to see all this in practice as we read in Daniel 1:4, *"Children in whom was no blemish, but well favoured, and skillful in all* **wisdom,** *and cunning in* **knowledge,** *and* **understanding** *in science, and such as had ability in them to stand in the king's palace."* You remember this great Bible story, do you not?

God gives it if man is in position to receive it and to use it for His glory!

Later on we hear that abilities in the skills of art, engraving, cutting of jewels, metal work, wood work, embroidery, and other skills given by God all come from **wisdom**. So can your ability to improve your teaching.

How do we get this? We get it by communicating to our great God that we want it *(prayer is asking and receiving)*. How do we communicate to God? We call it praying. And remember our initial challenge in this chapter – "You must pray to have your prayers answered!" Simple is it not, but *yet profound in its results!*

Concerning your **"alone time"** with God, *Dr. Tom Neal* in his well done book called *What You Don't Know About Prayer,* gives us a glimpse of several Bible personalities and their time alone with the Father.

"Jacob was alone with God. . . Genesis 32:24 – Elijah, I Kings 17:2-3; Daniel

10:2 – John the Baptist, *Luke 11:1, 'And it came to pass, that, as he was praying in a certain place, when he ceased, one of his disciples said unto him, Lord, teach us to pray, as John also taught his disciples.'* What a compliment! When the disciples asked Jesus to teach them to pray, they asked Him to teach them as John taught his disciples because they had seen answers to those prayers. They saw God do something, and they wanted to learn how to pray like that."

In this section he also added the prayer life of Jesus and Paul, with a good look at their results. This part alone is worth the price of the book as Dr. Neal helps us see the urgency of the *"alone time"* and getting answers from God!

A Review Of Key Thoughts:

The Spirit Of God In Your Teaching:

1. What does it mean to listen to the Spirit of God as you choose your content?

_____

_____

2. What does it mean to give the Spirit of God liberty in your presentation time?

_____

_____

3. What does it mean to allow the Spirit to close out your class?

_____

_____

The Prayer Life Of The Teacher:

1. To have your prayers answered you must do what? _____ (just one word)

2. Do you remember some of the values in the Discipleship Roll Book?

_____

_____

Chapter SIX

The Teacher's Time Of Presentation!

The week of preparation prepares you for the time of presentation. You begin with great faith in God. Because of your faith, you also anticipate life-change.

What does it take for you to become a specialist with your age group? You need to be effective.

The mannerisms you use in teaching will amount to 93% of what is actually communicated. On the other side, the student's mannerisms tell you all you need to know.

VI. The Teacher's Time of Presentation

1. Faith And Anticipation

2. Where Is The Passion, Compassion, And The Urgency?

3. Develop Into A Specialist With Your Age Group!

4. Compel, Persuade, And Encourage!

5. The Teacher's Mannerisms

6. The Student's Mannerisms Are Showing Too!

7. What Will Your Students Do Besides Just Sit There?

VI. The Teacher's Time of Presentation

1. Faith And Anticipation

Just as we have faith in our wonderful Savior to do all that He has promised to do, so do we put our trust in the written Word to do its work in the heart of the student.

What a great feeling it is to be used of God *"To so clarify what God has to say to the student, that the student could not possibly miss what God has to say to him."* That is a very large role to play for your church! Every teacher must accept the responsibility or not teach. Everything in this book relies on the development of the teacher's God-given gifts and the study and prayers we make as we trust God to use us.

It is not us and it is Him! It is not our Word and it is His! However, God has chosen someone like you who will pay the price to be prepared. This is where faith and works are both a necessity. What a marvelous privilege that our Heavenly Father will use us. Never abuse such an honor.

We can experience faith the whole week before our lesson. Pray in faith, by name, and by need. Use the **Discipleship Roll Book** to push yourself to make this happen consistently each week. Use the discipleship pages to remind yourself of who each student is and where they are coming from.

Ask earnestly that the Spirit of God would impress you throughout this week. See more ideas on this in the previous chapter. He is where the power is!

Pray in faith, by name, and by need.

Now, you are into the hour of presentation and the work of the Holy Spirit of God is not over. You need Him throughout your presentation to not only remind you as you proceed, but also to "break into" your lesson along the way. He can impress someone to say what would become the perfect addition to your own words. He can illuminate the minds of students to see themselves in the truth you teach.

Wow! What a partner who can work on the "inside" while you minister on the "outside." So, during your whole week of preparation you welcome the Spirit of God to impress you, guide you, and teach you. Then, during your hour of presentation you do not inform the Spirit of God that you can "handle it" from here on. You welcome His presence, His power, His fullness to control you from start to finish. Trust Him! Anticipate His involvement!

2. Where Is The Passion, Compassion, And the Urgency?

It is a fair question. You are not responsible for the class down the hallway, but you are for your classroom. With little to no contact with your students, you will probably never feel the passion, compassion, or the urgency of this lesson's truth for them. The lack of these true feelings shows up immediately in the lack of prayer for those you teach, the lack of connection, and the lack of preparation.

Do you feel much better when the class is over? Then you probably have no intentions of even glancing at next week's lesson until Thursday night at best. These areas of passion, compassion, and urgency are best described as non-existent. Would Jesus teach like you teach? Is He very pleased with both the attitude and action that is yours right now?

The dictionary uses Jesus Christ as the first example of passion. Passion is associated with emotions of "hate, love, grief, joy, intense emotional excitement, and also enthusiasm, affection, or strong desire." So, where is the passion associated with the life-changing possibilities of God's Word?

There are a few over forty Scripture references with the actual word of compassion. Almost every verse refers directly to our compassion upon another. The Lord is full of compassion:

"The Lord is gracious, and full of compassion; slow to anger, and of great mercy." Psalm 145:8
"And Jesus, moved with compassion. . ." Mark 1:41
"But when he saw the multitudes, he was moved with compassion." Matthew 9:36

As teacher, there must be urgency. For that **child** who may never hear you teach again, there must be some passion. For that **teenager** who may be filled with thoughts of rejecting the church just as soon as possible. For that **adult** who has promised God to give over that very area of life, but he never has.

God's judgment is extremely close. That student needs a teacher with great urgency.

As Paul wrote to Timothy, we see a glimpse of his passion: ***"To Timothy, my dearly beloved son: Grace, mercy, and peace, from God the Father and Christ Jesus our Lord. I thank God, whom I serve from my forefathers with pure conscience, that without ceasing I have remembrance of thee in my prayers, night and day; Greatly desiring to see thee, being mindful of thy tears. . ."***

Because of Paul's great compassion for Timothy, he then could address his young convert with tough answers about life: "endure hardness, be strong, study, shun profane and vain babblings, flee youthful lusts, follow righteousness, be gentle to all men, in meekness." Then, he lists twenty areas to avoid in II Timothy 3:2-5.

Passion: Never Teach Another Day Without It!

Now, let me address some practical thoughts about passion and how it can move us to study more, pray more, prepare more, and deliver the message with great care and urgency.

Let us define what it is: Passion is intense emotional excitement. It is strong love or affection. This word *intense* seems to capture the strength of strong passion. So it should be in our lives as we burn from within with a passion for the ability to teach as one who has the hand of God upon him. It is that great intensity that we are fully capable of having and that will help us to push ourselves.

It is that inside drive that just does not go away. Failure or success, it keeps bringing us back, with achievement on our mind. It is what I am willing to spend the rest of my life doing week in and week out. I know that because it is where the fulfillment comes from.

Have you and I experienced such fervor before for our passion? Am I so passionate about that dream I have had for many years that it would push me when I get down, encourage me when I falter, and drive me every day to finish the next step?

What would it take for me to back off, or let the fire of passion subside? If you had a very bad day of unpreparedness as a teacher, would it bother you?

Passion is sacrifice. It takes concentration and time and effort to arouse and to keep the fire within ablaze. *Sacrifice your mind from unproductive things.* No, not a kind of personal torture that must "dog" you every day of the week. But, those we hear about, read about, those who obviously have spent their life in a worthwhile cause, have also chosen to sacrifice some things for the sake of better things. Those things that arouse passion are definitely the better things. I trust that teaching God's Word is very high on your list!

> *What would it take to let the fire of passion subside?*

A passion for your ministry will need a time slot of your mind to stay fresh. A time set to dream some more dreams, to envision how to reach those dreams. *Remind yourself often of what your results may be and your passion increases.* Failure to do so may see your passion decline.

Sacrifice is not bad, it is good. You are *pushing yourself.* You are taking control of where your mind spends its time, and you are focusing more time on the things that bring you closer to success! When success is seen as coming closer and closer, passion seems to become more intense. It "winds my clock."

Sacrifice your time and effort. Anything worthy in life will take both your time and effort. But, if it is to achieve your goal, then that is one of the best uses of time and effort!

If you are a teacher now, a better lesson presentation will probably require better preparation (time and effort). If you want to be a better communicator than you are now, it will take more practice (time and effort). Some who have lost their passion seem to shun improvement. If they teach second graders, for example, they have not read a book on that age group in ten years. The passion is just not there. Not just for personal fulfillment, but neither for their students. The *push* is just not there like it used to be.

Passion welcomes self-discipline. **"Passion is fuel that drives performance. But without discipline, passion is just loud talk and noise. Passionate people who lack discipline will end up in life exactly where they began."** Sanborn, *Encore Effect.*

Personal discipline is so easy to talk about, because we all know it is a must, but hard to undertake for a lifetime. Those who have undertaken the effort to keep striving to a greater level of achievement than is the *"run of the mill"* are the ones we all read about. They have paid the price. They knew what the price was and have spent their time paying for it.

Passion gives you positive energy for the long run. *"Your positive energy and vision must be greater than anyone's negativity. Your confidence must be greater than everyone's doubt."* Jon Gordon, *The Energy Bus.*

Even when you fail along the way, the passion does not subside; it pulls your emotions together to remember the goal that is still there on the *inside*. In his unique book entitled *Jump Start Your Brain,* Doug Hall reminds us how to cope with the setbacks along the way. **"Recognize that when one of your ideas fails, it's not a reflection on 'you.' It's a reflection on 'it.' Failure is part of the process of learning. Your best teachers are your mistakes."** Mr. Hall's follow-up book *Jump Start Your Business Brain* is even better!

3. Develop Into A Specialist With Your Age Group!

Passion will soar higher as you become a specialist. You are gifted. Then, you have risen to a higher level of gifts, from your years of practice, training, and experiences. After years, for some of you, you have "honed" those gifts to a much higher and more valuable level of use than ever before. *Are you in the best place for the results from your gifts and abilities?* After forty years of ministry, I am convinced that some teachers should never teach. The fire is not there now, nor has it ever been. You may have been in a church where they begged for teachers *(forget the usual requirements for teachers, we will take anyone.)* The agreement was for you to teach for six weeks, "just until we find the permanent teacher." That was *"baloney"* from the start. That was seven years ago and not one candidate has yet to be interviewed. Find that place where you would rather be, and go for it! Some singers should only sing in the shower. Excuse me. Some who work with adults should work with teens or vice versa. Working to improve your gifts in one area leads to becoming a specialist. That is what churches need!

Winston Churchill said a lot of motivating things and lived a highly motivated life. He was awarded the Nobel Peace Prize for literature in 1953 for his book *The Second World War.* He said, "There's a special moment in everyone's life, a moment for which that person was born. That special opportunity, when he seizes it, will fulfill his mission – a mission for which he is uniquely qualified. In that moment, he finds greatness. It is his finest hour."

Become that specialist where God has given the opportunity. Refuse graciously, but refuse to sign up for every new job at church because no one else will. Let the professional "pew-sitters" do something. You protect that ministry that God is asking you to be great in. You have one life and this is it. You will never relive yesterday no matter how hard you try. Be your absolute best for God before you go to meet your God!

One of the joys of life is in finding that perfect spot for the work of which you are most gifted. Why would you desire a week longer to spend the rest of

your life in an area, while another area would be the absolute ideal for you and your abilities? Would not your passion be greater in the very spot you wish you were in all the time? It seems like the best way to relight the passion! Everyone has a place where they add the most value. Are you in that perfect place? Push yourself to get there quickly.

> *Are you in the perfect place to serve the Lord best? Why not?*

Tom Newberry in his book entitled *Success Is Not An Accident* reminds us, "Americans have been misled into believing they will not be held accountable for their choices and that they will miraculously harvest something other than what they planted. I call this the Big Lie. This dangerously popular distortion promotes mediocrity and underachievement."

What is it you enjoy talking about all the time? What is the subject you seem almost like an expert on? That will probably be close to your passionate area. What area of church ministries is that? Is that where you spend your time? It should be for that is where God could make you a specialist for the cause of Christ!

4. Compel, Persuade, And Encourage!

This is how Jesus approached men and women. It is how Paul ministered. Thus, it is an example to us as to how we are to present the truth to our students.

These words describe the end-intent of our words used earlier of passion, compassion, and urgency. If these are true within us as the teacher, then the lesson should conclude with a strong compelling, persuading, and encouraging of our students to believe, receive, and to practice God's wonderful Word. An agreement with truth as the best way to live and honor God does not necessarily translate into life change.

No, our role is not to "talk them into a decision," such as through sixteen verses of *"Just As I Am."* I have seen this happen back in the "hills," when men and women literally pulled others from the pews to "pray through." There was no Bible opened, no counsel or verses given. The prospect had no clue as to what happened.

We are not advocating this type of compelling or persuading, but the student often needs to understand that the time is urgent. *"Then Agrippa said unto Paul, Almost thou persuadest me to be a Christian," Acts 26:28. "Knowing therefore the terror of the Lord, we persuade men. . ." II Corinthians 5:11.*

Anticipation brings good thoughts of good results to come. With such an anticipation of spiritual results to take place within the classroom, it will show on the face of the teacher and in her mannerisms. There will be a bubbling passionate voice, eyes wide open, gestures full of expression, and several plans to involve the student in active listening. This teacher is ready to take step one toward the lesson goal!

John Maxwell says in *Everyone Communicates, Few Connect*, "What do I want them to know? And what do I want them to do? If I have clear answers to those two questions, then I am much more likely to stay on track, get to the point, and connect with my listeners."

"The achievement of personal excellence is a decision you make- or that you fail to make. But in the absence of a commitment to excellence in your chosen field, you automatically default to average performance- or even mediocrity." Brian Tracy **"No Excuses."**

5. The Teacher's Mannerisms

You are up front! Everyone is looking in your direction (hopefully). You are the key to dictate the pattern for the student's mannerisms. Do not let that scare you, for it is how everyone "comes across" as we try to communicate.

In this chapter, let us try to see just how significant your mannerisms are to your classroom and to your own ability to communicate. Then, let us act on some of the suggestions if they are missing at present in your teaching.

Wesley Willis said, "Usually, class interaction and participation is at its greatest level during the 'preliminaries.' But, when the teacher stands up, the student's involvement in the class comes screeching to a stop." *Make Your Teaching Count*

a. Mannerisms are major in communication

In these forty years of being around teachers, actually thousands of them in two large churches and training sessions for all these years, the variety of teacher mannerisms are too numerous to number. Most are somewhat good, some in dire need, and in others it is just sad.

Every teacher will not be like the most vivacious you have seen. Some will be best at voice inflection, some by their energetic gestures and story telling, while others it just seems to be their dynamic personality. However "dry" you may seem to be at this time, dynamics can be learned and practiced.

> *The goal of improvement for a teacher never ends, never!*

Then, there are those who can read a Bible passage or story with a "stone face." There seems to be no facial expressions, only slow-motion gestures, with a lack of enthusiasm or emotion in their voice. No matter how good the content is planned, the implementation of this great truth lost something during the delivery time. The lesson died, and so did the hope for life-change. Teaching does not have to go on and on without improvements. That is why you are reading this book. You desire to improve your ability. The goal of improvement for a teacher never ends, never!

God has gifted you for this high calling of being a teacher. But, original gifts, never developed to their highest level of perfection, are like "putting the gifts of God on hold."

Some of the most enthusiastic teachers I have ever met are in their late seventies to early eighties. They are still teaching, still reading, still trying something new. They look at every piece of display materials I bring, and for the next four hours of training just cannot seem to get enough.

Other teachers seem to stay about thirty feet away from the nearest teacher aid. I spend four hours setting up the auditorium with visual aids and books, and yet some never walk up to even take a look. That is sad.

b. Take a wide-open look at mannerisms

Let us look now at some of the stats we find that will bring life to your classroom, and almost all are dependent upon the teacher.

The largest study concerning communication, and still in college textbooks today, give us the findings. *What actually comes across:*

> *(1) By Words Alone*..*7%*

> *(2) By Tone of Voice*...*38%*

> *(3) By Facial Expressions & Gestures*.................*55%*

> **Dr. Albert Mehrabian**

Here we see what thousands of Bible teachers have never heard or realized, that **93% of communication** is actually above and beyond the words you say! Communication here is about **what actually comes across to the student.**

For many of us, that is hard to believe. Because we are prejudice, we do not want to know that all the great words and phrases we use are not all there is to bringing the truth across.

However, we must see how significant the 93% is in communicating the Word of God. We can improve on that part and should keep on getting better as a teacher for our Lord!

In his good book *How Do I Get These Kids To Listen,* Evangelist Ed Dunlop, reminds us of the over-whelming value of your own voice in teaching: "YOUR VOICE – What a powerful, versatile and dynamic teaching tool God gave you when he equipped you with a voice! The human voice has more versatility and possibilities than a grand piano. That voice box of yours can produce shouts, whispers, grunts, groans, wails, sobs, laughter and shrieks of joy, anger, insecurity, hatred, love, suspicion, enthusiasm, confidence, scorn, and admiration. What an instrument! What a tool for capturing and holding attention!"

c. Practice your mannerisms

Take a five minute portion of your lesson or story, stand before a full mirror and present your thought or story. Watch your facial features. Does your face express the words you are saying? Now, do it again and watch your hands and body movement. Now again, and listen to your voice. Did your voice compliment the strong emotional words you

Does your face express the words you are saying?

used?

The next time you watch a dramatic program on TV (not sitcoms, please), watch a good actor for all of the above traits of good communication.

Ask a friend-teacher to critique you as you practice telling a story or giving an illustration. Then, let your friend practice while you critique her. Help each other to improve.

Set up a video in the back of your classroom, then, when no one is around, lock all the doors, pull the blinds and watch yourself (as your students do each week). You may quickly pick up on some little annoying habits you have. See yourself looking to one side far more than the other. You tap your pen on the table at least seventy-five times each week. You had no idea that your students are counting the "taps" weekly to see if you break your old record! Your eye contact is on the wall or out the window or on a chair where nobody is sitting. You say "Uhhh" about fifty times, which the students are counting too.

In other words, it is also possible for the teacher to be the greatest distraction of all. You need to know that.

Three months later, review yourself again to see if you have improved. These are some of the "above average" improvements that only *above average teachers* make. They are putting genuine effort into becoming a better teacher for God!

The teacher controls how the classroom goes. It is under your management! Probably, most students, even adults will arrive with no idea of the lesson for this week. They have not studied one verse in preparation and probably have not prayed much either.

Here are the other areas in need of a decision by the teacher:

Subject Matter:	*Teacher Style:*	*Presentation You Give:*
Words you will use	Methods you will use	Choice of dress
Verses you choose	Use visuals or not	Formal or relaxed
To go in depth or skim over	Lecture on involvement	Stern or positive
What is emphasized	Stand, sit, move around	Tone of voice
What is neglected	Use emotion or "blah"	Facial expressions
To illustrate or not		Eye contact

The teacher makes these decisions before teaching begins. You have a very responsible role to play for the Lord. You are a teacher for God!

Never forget that approximately 93% of communication (what actually comes across) is above and beyond the words you say. It is HOW you say what you say that makes the dramatic difference between one class to the next.

It is possible for the teacher to be the greatest distraction of all!

d. Practice the words you say
Practice on a Bible verse like **Genesis 6:5,** **"And God saw that the wickedness of man was great in the earth, and that every imagination of the thoughts of his heart was only evil continually."**

Wow! Strong emotional words we see that God used to express what He saw in man on the earth. WICKEDNESS – EVIL. These are not your "run of the mill" words found in most sentences. God calls sin "evil" and "wickedness." Look at the extent of this sin as God grabs our attention: "every imagination of the thoughts of his heart was only evil continually." Whoa! You cannot possibly miss how God feels about this situation, thus came the flood of judgment.

However, the student could pass right on by without feeling such significance of what man is capable of if the teacher passes on by also. Sometimes, we need to pause a bit, slow it down, or as the Bible says often, *Selah!*

Expression "paints the picture" in the mind of the student. They must see the full emotional intent of God's Word. Do it justice, express it strongly when needed. Now, you do not have to pronounce evil or wickedness in a sinister or *"hissing from hell"* sound, but words like this do demand a stronger expression than the average sentence. Watch for words such as: adversary – affliction – anger/angry – backslidden – bitterness – blasphemy – carnal – chasten – corrupt – darkness – defile – despise – enemy – foolishness – hell – perish – transgressions – and so many more. Slow down when you meet up with those strong emotional words, think them through, then properly express them so students could not possibly miss what God intended to say. That is who you are and what you do!

Other words may be in a context of positive or negative. Make sure your students know the difference between the good or the bad of *"everlasting life"* or the great sin problem of *"everlasting punishment."* Show and express the great difference between *faith and faithless.* Watch also for verses with an *"if"* that brings with it a wonderful promise for the believer "If" you do whatsoever I command you. That is a big little word and should be expressed so!

For those of you who teach children, please understand that storytelling is a super place to get your lesson intent into the mind of the child. It becomes the most remembered part of your lesson. Kids and even eighty-five year old kids can remember the story for weeks and even years ahead. Then, if you put the truth inside the story, they take them both home.

Behavior, under control, always seems it is best during the story or illustration you tell. Storytelling brings the truth into real life. Great communicators have mastered the art of storytelling. It works from the tiny tots to the most elderly of your church family. Your elderly folks live much of their lives now on the stories of the past, their personal life and experiences. Listen to their conversation. Most are bringing up something from the past – stories. They love stories. The truth of God, set in a real life scenario is the best for clarifying your lesson point.

Storytelling brings the truth into real life – the student's real life!

Let us look now at what happens in your classroom that the teacher, not the student is in charge of.

e. The lesson content:
You, not the student, will need to care for the words to be used, and the verses to be used in the lesson. In other words, the selector is you. Will you go in depth or just skim over some words and verses? What will be emphasized and what will be neglected? To illustrate once, twice, three times, or not to illustrate. The teacher controls all of the above, not the student.

From the book *Mastering Teaching* by Palmer, Hestenes, Hendricks: "People want to see themselves; their dreams, their needs, their problems and their heartbreaks. Nothing moves listeners more than their reality, their experience, their emotions, and their struggles. They don't want to hear something brand new as much as something relevant to them. They want to feel *this teacher understands me.*"

f. The teacher's style:

The methods you intend to use this week are all up to you. Whether you use visuals or not is your job too. Will it be a total lecture, or will you plan classroom involvement? Will you stand, sit, or move around? Will you prepare visuals? Will you mark the places

you need to have strong emotion or just read that verse in an average conversational tone? Will you talk fast, slow, loud?

All of the above falls under your role of teacher. Most of your students have no idea what the lesson is even about. It is your move. It seems like your role of teaching becomes more significant as we go!

g. Your mannerisms are showing!

What will be your choice of dress? Will you be rather formal or relaxed? Will you be stern or positive, or a plan for both? Did you bring your best facial expressions this week? And here is a biggie – eye contact! If you are actually pretty bad with eye contact, work on it. On your page of notes, to the side, every three inches draw an eye, or print EC. As you scan your notes from time to time this will remind you to look at a student. Before long it has now become your "style" of teaching and you will not need the little eyes all over your page!

When I first went back to college at age 29, just married, in my second semester, I had a speech class. I already knew from the first semester that reading or speaking aloud was bad news for me. Back in the hills you did not talk all that much, except to your dog. But, it came time for a ten minute speech. I was actually ready for the speech. I had it memorized. I had practiced at home many times. I sat in the class with six young "post high school kids" just coming to college. At twenty-nine years old, I was older than the teacher.

We stood in a carpeted room but on a small wooden podium to speak. When my turn came, I was already sweating big time. Large drops of water were already on my forehead. I got two minutes into my ten minute speech and "the lights were flashing, but the train wasn't coming." It was over. I could not literally get a word to cross my lips. I knew exactly what to say, I could see the words in my mind. I could form my mouth to say the word, but nothing came out. The sweat enlarged.

The absolute truth – I stood there for eight very long minutes with nothing to say. I could not even say "Uhhhh." The rule was that you did not sit down until the time was up. Those little kids sat there trying to keep from laughing, and me, a grown man, trying to keep from crying. Ohhh, it was bad. I looked over at the teacher, and even he was laughing.

Then came the final touch. The sweat on my brow was now so heavy, that is was not just rolling down my body any more, the drops were so big now that they dropped from my forehead down to the wooden podium, and you could hear the drops hit. That did it. Finally, the teacher said, **"Time!"**

That day was a day that I learned how to plan a campaign of self-improvement.

I then got a man to sit down and listen as I read. Then, I graduated to a small group of people to listen as I read. Gradually it worked itself out.

Perhaps there is some area that is really in need of some work. Find it and fix it!

Remember, you (as the teacher) are the only one who can make your classroom a place where students could learn if they would learn. Perhaps your preparation time needs to add one or two hours per week to get where you need to be.

You can improve yourself to the status of excellence, but not without the effort. Do not allow "Negative Ned" or "It Won't Work Wilma" to talk you out of improving. They actually believe they are not creative like others, with no possibility to become creative. Nonsense! Those type attitudes deserve my severest comments: "BALONEY!" I learned that good word even as a child. I would complain about my chores and Dad would say, "Son, that's a bunch of baloney." I knew exactly what he said.

We have centered our thoughts here more on the teacher, or your person. How you make eye contact, your total facial features, your gestures, body actions or reactions, tone of voice, all will make up you the teacher.

Later, as we discuss methods and techniques, visual tools, and all that captures their attention, we will find that in reality those are mannerisms too. They become your "manner" or style. They make you the teacher that

> *Learn to "read" individuals.*

you are. That is why others cannot wait to be promoted to your class!

6. The Student's Mannerisms Are Showing Too!

Before we end our session on mannerisms, here is an idea that helps you greatly. As it is true for a teacher that "your mannerisms are showing," so it is true that the mannerisms of your students may be clearly seen by the teacher.

Learn to "read" individuals, as well as the whole class in general. With *children*, they rarely try to hide their behavior, it just happens for all to see.

With *teen and adult* behavior they have learned along the way to become somewhat subtle about their own mannerisms. We have probably taught them to just sit and quietly listen. That is because other teachers have taught students to act nice while board stiff. Just sit through class again with your mind gone to lunch and watch the minute hand slowly creep towards time for the bell. They have learned to be polite. They see nothing, say nothing, and do nothing.

Make Your Teaching Count by Willis- "An effective learning environment cannot be characterized by learners sitting quietly in rows. It is also terribly important to realize that keeping learners quiet often has nothing to do with actually teaching them."

7. What Will Your Students Do Besides Just Sit There?

It is what happens every Sunday across America. Children, teens, and adults in many classes just sit there and listen without any kind of involvement, not even a question. Not always, but far too often it happens. How is it in your class?

It is certainly not because the Word of God we teach is non-transforming in lives. It is often because they have heard the same passage before (content) several times, but the relevancy was weak or absent.

That is why the research on over 1000 former Sunday School students now in their twenties from churches like yours and mine no longer attend their church. Their reason being the lack of relevancy. They even believe that God's Word is true, they have just never seen it connect to real life. When confronted in the real world where they live each week or in school, they have few answers for life.

As teacher, you must see the value of less total content and more connection through definitions of words, discussions, role plays, illustrations, logical sequence, visuals that aid retention, all coming from a well prayed, well prepared, compassionate teacher filled with a great passion for teaching and filled with the Spirit of God.

Wow! That is a mouthful of potentiality. But, our dear Lord is full of the power to develop any and all potential within us.

Did you ever think in your high school years of classes why many tests given seemed "so useless" for your future career? Why did we memorize so many lists that we have never used one time since? How many note pages in college have I never looked at since? It was all a form of testing or evaluating whatever learning is supposed to have taken place. Looking back, now that I have personally taught a college course and prepared tests; I can see the only reasoning for some of those tests was for "easy grading."

In the book *Endangered Minds,* Healy writes, "What was educationally significant and hard to measure has been replaced by what is educationally insignificant and easy to measure. So now we measure how well we've taught what isn't worth learning!"

Whoops! Did you ever read something so bad that was so true?

Content makes us knowledgeable. Application makes it understandable enough to change our lives.

Watch your time carefully, allowing for the "Big Five," if you deem it appropriate!

A Review Of Key Thoughts:

1. There is something for our class that we should never teach another day without:

P_____

2. One of the quotes from *Encore Effect* states, "Passionate people who lack

_____ will end up in life exactly where they began."

3. Are you in the perfect place to serve the Lord best with your giftedness?

Yes _____ No _____ If not, why not? _____

_____

If not, what is your plan? _____

_____

4. As a teacher, what does it mean to *Compel – Persuade – Encourage* your students?

_____

5. _____% of communication is actually above and beyond the words you say!

6. In your classroom, regardless of ages, what do your students do besides just sit there?

_____

_____

Chapter SEVEN

Application Is Why You Teach - Don't Leave Home Without It.

Application is why you teach. Without application there is no possibility of life-change. Application means applied to life. Step 3 and 4 of the Learning Process is application! Without it, do not expect life-change. At least half of your lesson time should see you out of content and into the application of the content!

VII. Application Is Why We Teach!

1. A Couple Of Misconceptions

2. Content Is A Goal, But Not The Higher Goal

3. Life-Change Is The Higher Level Of Learning

4. Life-Change Comes From The Scriptures

5. Our Rally Cry Is To "Do It"

6. Application Is Taught With Passion

7. Application Demands Building Need For The Lesson!

8. Grab Their Attention, Or Application Does Not Matter

9. Felt Needs And Real Needs Are Many

10. Application Needs to "Fit" Your Students

11. Why Teach This Lesson? The Goal Is Always Life-Change!

VII. Application Is Why We Teach!

1. A Couple Of Misconceptions

(a) The reason we teach a lesson is to explain the quarterly or our contents and to cover all we intended to cover. ***WRONG!***

(b) Our thinking more often starts and stops with content. Thus, we conclude that a lot of content will lead to understanding. ***WRONG!***

Content does not change lives unless you are even more thorough with application that shows the truth in real life. Why have students heard the same truth you are teaching today from 15-25 times or more in their past and still do not live that way today? I firmly believe that many students never go home and think it through again to see how it works in "street clothes" or "inside their own house." It just does not "hit home" during the class time, and so it fades quickly away.

That is why Step 3 of the Learning Process is to **Personalize**. Spend no time in personalizing the truth into their real life and they too often go home with no complete understanding, thus, no application.

As you approach your lesson you realize that content is good, but **it is not good enough.** Think of your own response to messages over the years. You hear a message, you agree with it, but it changes nothing in your life style. In fact, you have heard that same truth at least 75 times in the last twenty years.

Like you, just hearing it again is not enough. You need to *recognize yourself* in that truth. As teacher, you may see it immediately, but several of your students will miss it every time. **Application is your role as teacher,** to make sure they do not miss it. Look for the "real life application" in every lesson you teach. Take nothing for granted – assume nothing!

2. Content Is A Goal, But Not The Higher Goal

Be careful not to look on the accumulation of content as the major goal. The content of God's Word is a goal and a good one, but not the life-change-today goal. To know more and more about the Bible is a goal, but not like the immediate, urgent goal that could change your obedience today!

> *Look for the "real life application" in every lesson you teach.*

The more you study at home, in Bible class, and in church, you will know more and more about the Bible. But that is a life-long goal. You want to be a life-long learner. But along with that happening every time I teach, I also want to see real lives hear the truth that could change them before the class is dismissed. *That is the higher level of learning!*

3. Life-Change Is The Higher Level Of Learning

The proof of the lesson learned is in the **action**, which is a change in attitude about the truth and in lifestyle.

Living for Christ is not something you "ought to do;" it is something that you do. It is an action; it is doing; it is an experience of bringing your life into compliance with the Word of God.

I believe, perhaps unaware, we actually train our students to just sit quietly, look straight ahead without bothering the teacher. Thus, we literally teach students to just sit there and wait until the guy is through. Just keep looking at your watch and he will be through in a few minutes.

How about trying another approach for the next two weeks. Next Sunday, our lesson is this . . . **"Be ye kind one to another. . ." Ephesians 4:32.** Prepare yourself to describe what this looks like, to define the verse. So, your actual student involved lesson for Sunday is to plan out this verse in real life for the week ahead. In class you will brainstorm your students for their ideas as to how to live this way in their home. Discuss the ideas given.

Set a goal: Do three kind acts this week without anybody knowing it was you. Your objective is to choose one or two ideas to practice this week.

Next week's class time: your lesson will be to review the truth once again, then, the bulk of the class will be consumed as students testify of the week of living in obedience to God's Word!

What do you think? Would that be considered a non-spiritual class since the teacher did not get to talk the whole time? I believe I can guess your answer.

From the book *Teaching For Results*, Findley Edge says, "When we take learning out of the normal experience of living and place it in the unnatural environment of a classroom, we often make learning unnatural also." The conclusion is for the teacher to bridge the gap between content and walking and talking the truth.

4. Life-Change Comes From The Scriptures

There is that great purpose for Scripture as we read in **II Timothy 3:16-17, "All scripture is given by inspiration of God, and is profitable for doctrine, for reproof, for correction, for instruction in righteousness: That the man of God may be perfect, throughly furnished unto all good works."**

Scripture is given for doctrine, reproof, correction, instruction; but is given for the purpose of *verse 17*, "That" in verse 17 is now introducing what all of the above was given for. It is for the purpose: *"that the man of God may be perfect,"* or complete.

Many students know already that they *"should"* live like that before they walked in your classroom door. Now, you just taught them again that they *"should"* live that way. However, without the application of *HOW* to live that way, it is simply another lesson of many on *"you ought to."* Most students already know that. They need to know the *HOW!* How much of that would they get in your classroom?

We teach children through our Bible Memory System that verses are for living: real life, neighborhood, school, playground type of living. It is a truth and agreed to that we "ought to live like that."

One set of ten verses for our 4th to 6th graders carries the theme of *"My Love For God."* For example, in Psalm 37:5, "Commit thy way unto the Lord; trust also in him; and he shall bring it to pass." The verse teaches *"My Commitment to God."* So, in ten verses this is what this one theme is teaching our children:

1. My Commitment To God – Psalm 37:5
2. My Faith In God – Hebrews 11:6
3. My Holiness To God – Romans 12:1
4. My Obedience To God – John 15:14
5. My Praise To God – Hebrews 13:15
6. My Reverence For God – Revelation 4:11
7. My Thankfulness To God – Psalm 100:4
8. My Trust In God – Proverbs 3:5
9. My Worship To God – Matthew 4:10
10. With All My Heart – Deuteronomy 6:5

In this one theme of ten verses we try to saturate a junior child's mind with

> *Saturate a junior child's mind with a reason he should express praise to His great God.*

a reason he should *express praise to his great God.* He needs to *say it and do it* in real life. Then, there are the projects in their Club book that help them to see how to express their love to God. Being a child of God is for real life living!

"For we are his workmanship, created in Christ Jesus unto good works, which God hath before ordained that we should walk in them." Ephesians

2:10

In our verse used previously *(II Timothy 3:16-17)* we see that truth in the light of *"action."* **"Perfect and furnished"** is for the purpose of doing *(action),* life-style living!

Let the Lord express it: "And why call ye me, Lord, Lord, and **do not** the things which I say?" Luke 6:46 *(emphasis added)*

"Thou hast commanded us to keep thy precepts diligently. O that my ways *(life styles)* were directed to keep thy statutes!" Psalm 119:4-5 **(parentheses added)**

As you teach and apply real life application, God will use you. The Spirit of God will work on the *"inside"* as you clarify the truth on the *"outside!"*

When the Judgment Seat of Christ rolls around to your turn, will His judgment be based on your clear understanding and agreement with the truth as stated, or upon your obedience?

Therefore, every lesson is significant: **"All Scripture"** . . . This means that whatever you teach in class this week from God's Word could have a long lasting real-life change upon anyone or all of your students.

Thus, my preparation, my prayers, my earnest desire is to see as much **application** as I see **content.** This becomes my passion for the next lesson.

Jesus reminds us again in the Great Commission verses, *"teaching them to observe all things. . ."* *(to do – to obey).* Sounds like application!

Application obviously needs to be appropriate for who you teach. Student needs should always be high on your list in determining the application you choose.

5. Our Rally Cry Is To "Do It!"

In the book *Why Nobody Learns Much Of Anything At Church,* Thom and Joani Schultz write, "And Jesus knew people learned by doing. To teach his disciples a lesson on servant-hood, he dropped to his knees and began washing their feet. He could have preached an eloquent sermon on servant-hood. But he knew the power of experience. He knew his men would best understand if they experienced this lesson."

Doing is the goal. When does the truth of God's Word transfer into real life change? (1) When time is left for a response back to God about the truth just heard. (2) When time is left for personal prayer (where commitment to God is made). (3) The teacher initiates application by persuading, suggesting, painting a positive picture of change, and encouraging students to choose what is right.

6. Application Is Taught With Passion

The teacher is in charge of the various application considerations, the exact time to respond to God's Word, and the only one in the class who can initiate this response time back to God.

Application cannot be left to the pastor alone, at the "official" church invitation time. Change can take place in your Sunday school class, before you dismiss, but not without the opportunity.

Teaching without application is fruitless. You never see any results. The closest comment you hear is *"that was a good lesson,"* end of discussion. To add to my life, or to get sin out of my life, there must be opportunity to respond to God.

I believe this is what our Lord is teaching us, as we review some verses:

Jesus said **"compel them to come in" Luke 14:23. "And the lord said unto the servant, Go out into the highways and hedges, and compel them to come in, that my house may be filled."**

When do we compel students? Remember the "almost" statement of King Agrippa: **"Then Agrippa said unto Paul, Almost thou persuadest me to be a Christian." Acts 26:28**

When do we persuade students?

The Lord makes it very clear in **II Corinthians 5:10-11, "For we must all appear before the judgment seat of Christ; that every one may receive the things done in his body, according to that he hath done, whether it be good or bad. Knowing therefore the terror of the Lord, we persuade men. . ."**

Paul sought to persuade King Agrippa. In Acts 26:28, Timothy had been "persuaded" by Paul. The dictionary defines this word with *"reason, urging, convince, or come to a conviction."*

God can still use us to persuade students as Jesus did and as Paul did. Where is that passion and drive that I started out with years ago?

The lack of emotional expression negates the force of persuasion. So, how do we persuade students? (1) By HOW you say what you say. Do you really mean it? Do your students believe you? (2) By your tone of voice. (3) Your eyes are most expressive of all. (4) Your facial expressions, gestures, etc. (5) Crystal clear words and terms.

You will likely say to yourself, *"I knew that already."* Yes, but when is the last time you taught like that? Over the years, even without reading you have picked up on good teaching methods and techniques, but where are they today?

The teacher must have purpose to *hit the mark*, not all around it. What am I walking into class to say? For what purpose am I studying and praying all week? When I have the purpose well defined, then I cannot but persuade my students to respond to God's Word!

For those of you who have the privilege to teach little bus children, you know quite well that you may only have one or two weeks to teach that child what he will never ever get at home. With his home life, he may be in front of you only a handful of times and never again. You need that passionate drive within you to not miss the target when "it" shows up!

7. Application Demands Building Need For The Lesson!

Again, the significance of the teacher demands he must take on some more responsibilities.

Although the teacher carries heavy-duty responsibilities, the Spirit of God is always there to help us have a creative class and to assure that learning could take place. We cannot make people learn, but they *could* learn if they *would* learn in our classroom!

The *teacher* is responsible for allowing enough time to apply the truth to real life. Your role is to so prepare, to adapt to the situation, so that students would literally refuse to learn in your classroom. This is the type of teacher that the dear Lord needs in every classroom, young or older. You have one of the most significant roles of all at church that carries the most significant results.

You must exercise *self-discipline* to improve yourself. Please stop taking on every new "need" within the church. There are plenty of others to take on those roles, for there will be many more pop up. Let others fill in there, including the "pew-sitters."

Do you need to put in any "extra" time to improving yourself? You cannot retain the same without fresh thoughts and new techniques. You learn those by reading, thinking, preparing new visuals, and trying new ideas. Spend your time there. Set your sights on becoming a *"specialist"* in children, or teens, or your age group of adults! God needs **outstanding** teachers! The fulfillment of teaching is so much more when you constantly improve yourself.

The teacher's role is not to blame the student for their distant looks, but to counter-act boredom, disinterest, and distractions of all kinds. That's why you must set aside time to improve yourself. After your first twenty years of teaching, your heart says, "I need more, I must have more knowledge for teaching God's Word!"

If the teacher is unaware that the lesson will "strike home" to the student, then just teach anything. It does not matter, they will probably need it anyway. But, that is why Step 3 in the Learning Process is to **Personalize.** Neglecting real needs may easily lend itself to disinterest *(they see no connection or need to listen.)* That leads to boredom, and open for the first distraction that comes along.

"The very way in which we view the world is called our perception. Our individual perception also determine our natural learning strengths, or learning styles. . . There are two perceptual qualities that each mind possesses. They are concrete perceptions (our five senses). The key phrase simply stated is 'It is what it is.' The abstract quality allows us to visualize, to conceive ideas, to understand or believe what we can't actually see. When we are using this abstract quality, we are using our intuition, our intellect, our imagination." *The Way They Learn* by Cynthia Ulrich Tobias

If you teach children or teens, reread a good list of characteristics for the age group you teach. It reminds you of why your students act the way they do. It will help you to see that a new technique would help them listen. You must feed yourself and keep yourself up-to-date.

The disinterest shown by facial features, wandering eyes, heads turning, yawning, stretching, etc. are all signs they still do not see the need to listen. Some authors tell us that at least a third of the time you spend on the whole lesson should be spent preparing your first 5-6 minutes. That is how important your time to grab their attention and establish the need for them to listen really is. So, how much time do you spend on that first 5-6 minutes of the lesson?

8. Grab Their Attention, Or Application Does Not Matter

Why should someone listen to you anyway? **Children** have lots of things to think about besides what you have to say. They think about the prizes coming in Children's Church. They draw pictures, disturb their neighbors, or play with something they brought in their pocket.

Teenagers have clothes, money, their peers, peer pressure, the opposite sex, cell phones, texting, or sports on their mind.

Adults have plenty too to occupy their mind. Last week's problems, next week's problems, teenagers, credit cards, and on the list goes.

The thought here is that every age is easily distracted, especially concerning spiritual teaching. Therefore, as a teacher for God, I must train myself to control my classroom.

> *I must train myself to control my classroom.*

We will discuss later the methods and techniques of creative teachers. We are talking about (1) Use true-life stories (2) Hypothetical illustrations (3) What if this happened to you? (4) At home illustrations (5) Question/Answers (6) Provocative statement (7) Current events (8) Pictures, overhead, power point, Velcro boards, handouts, marker board, visuals, object lessons, discussions, and much more.

Try something new, and it will solve one of your problems!

9. Felt Needs And Real Needs Are Many

Felt needs are what the student knows he has and would like help. It is an "on the surface" need, often seen publicly by others. A felt need is like this: when pastor gets up to speak and announces his topic for the day, I lean over to my spouse and say, "I wonder if George is here today, ha ha. Look back and see if he's here, Honey. If he's not here let's get him a tape, what do you say?" It is like everyone in church knows that preacher is talking about George. It is an obvious need. He knows it, his wife knows it, and perhaps half the church knows it.

Then, there are the other needs or hidden needs we call a "real need." These needs are sub-surface, trying to be kept hidden. The classic example would be the need of the lost church member. In larger churches, because of the amount of people, you see this quite often.

I will never forget the night that one of our most faithful men came forward during the invitation, looked me right in the eye and said, "I have never been saved." He had been in our church for ten years. He heard every message Dr. Lee Roberson preached for ten years. He carried a Bible larger than mine, tithed, heard all the great Bible teachers in those days, sang louder than most around him, and even took audit courses in the college just to learn more about the Bible. You would think, as I did, that he was genuinely saved. But, he knew and God knew that he had never received Jesus Christ. It was very well hidden. That is how people are, and that is how some of your students are.

You never know for sure who sits in front of you, but God does!

Spend much time on your introduction, so that even an unsaved man may see the need to listen well. You never know for sure who sits in front of you, but God does!

10. Application Needs To "Fit" Your Students

To the best of your ability, get to know your students. It helps greatly to determine the application for your class. Here are some advantages for you: (1) Now, the teacher can prepare a role-play for the Smith couple, who are seeing this same problem with their children at home. Then, a role-play is prepared to allow them to see some Biblical options from which to choose, and hear the comments from others who have already been there.

(2) Or, we can have a discussion about Joe's workplace. He loves the Lord, but does not know how to handle an unspiritual environment or co-workers and needs some ideas from others who have been there.

(3) Or, knowing the habits of teenagers today, the teacher will add comment into the lesson to grab their attention. A "what if this happened to you" can very quickly point to a scenario that almost all parents would recognize immediately. It takes that extra effort, but that is what a passionate teacher puts into their lesson preparation. Are you that extra-mile teacher? It is a big question to ask yourself.

Application needs to grab hold of the student's mind. That is why the process that could lead to life change includes the *Understanding* of the words and terms being discussed; the *Personalizing* that brings it "home" to the student; then to *Practice* shows how it looks in everyday life.

That is what the teaching techniques you use such as discussions, problem solving, what if this happened to you scenarios, and illustrations help students to see it in their life style! Use a brainstorm session to allow the students to verbalize what they see or feel in their mind.

Set up a weekly "Situation Room" in your lesson time. "Now class, let's take this same truth to the 'Situation Room.' Joe, you work five days a week in a tough environment for a Christian. How do you see this truth working in your life on the job? Sue, you are a nurse facing life and death on any day at the hospital. You know this truth from God is true, so, is there any way or opportunities to apply this truth in your situations? Terry and Jane, you have four children at home. By implementing this truth into your home life, how would it apply to kids?"

So, with your marker board, set up a special place in your room where you walk to and engage the "Situation Room." Just by changing their eye sight to a different spot grabs their attention anew. It initiates the minds of your students to transform themselves from the Bible truth to the Bible truth in their real everyday life!

Your lesson content can easily blend into real life. It will take some discipline on your part to "pick and choose" the best 40-50% of the best content in front of you. Remember, it is not all the most significant for your class. Some content needs to be discarded for the "best out of all the rest."

For example, here is how I would break down a lesson that could go in many directions; but the goal is one truth thoroughly taught. The skeleton outline is shown below, then a few comments will help you see this example.

Lesson: Escaping Temptation I Corinthians 10:13

I. (7 min.) "There hath no temptation taken you but such as is common to man. . ."

TYPES OF TEMPTATION/ BIBLICAL EXAMPLES

1. The "worldly lusts"- Titus 2:12
2. The "flesh" sins - Galatians 5:19-21
3. The "lust of the eyes" - I John 2:16

II. (10 min.) ". . . but God is faithful, who will not suffer (allow) you to be tempted above that ye are able. . ."

BIBLICAL EXAMPLES/ GOD'S FORGIVENESS

1. _____ 1. _____
2. _____ 2. _____
3. _____ 3. _____

III. (25 min.) ". . . but will with the temptation also make a way to escape, that ye may be able to bear it." I Corinthians 10:13

WAYS TO ESCAPE:

1. _____ 4. _____
2. _____ 5. _____
3. _____ 6. _____

Response time to God: Would you right now in these last few minutes of class, respond to the Lord about one of these problem areas or other specific needs you presently face? *(Allow a response time now!)*

An explanation: Most all of your students already understand temptation, sin, and forgiveness of sins. However, churches are filled with Christians who still, even after years of your teaching, still have "secret" sins that they cannot seem to get rid of. They cannot seem to "make a way to escape."

I would spend about seven minutes on point 1 because every person already knows what it is to be tempted. They were tempted this week and the week before and perhaps were tempted even not to come to church today. However, I would remind them briefly of some types of temptations and give a quick Bible example of the temptations that often led to sin in Bible times.

But then, move on to point 2; and here is where I would spend a little more time giving two or three Bible examples of God's great forgiveness when we do fall. It is encouragement that the Lord is always there, willing and able to forgive sins.

Point 3 is where I then would spend the bulk of my time dealing with the solution that God promises, "a way to escape." That is where most of us seem to have the problem of sins that keep on returning – we do not seem to be able to escape them. Let us spend our time there!

Whenever the topic or emphasis is given to you for the next week, you need to begin early to make your decision of content to keep and content to toss. Toss it without regret. Too many teachers come to class with too much stuff. Both the teacher and for sure the students suffer. Generalities about many points lead to no specific decision made on any.

11. Why Teach This Lesson? The Goal Is Always Life-Change!

When you teach for this purpose it will decide the amount and the selection of the content you use.

Jesus used Scriptures that *"hit home"* to those who listened. Remember the Learning Process and Step 3, **To Personalize.**

"For *thou* has had five husbands; and he whom *thou* now hast is not. . ."

"Wilt *thou* be made whole?"

"But there are *some of you* that believe not."

"*He* that is without sin among you, let *him* cast the first stone."

> *Jesus used Scripture that "hit home" to those who listened.*

Jesus **personalized** the truth to where the student could not possibly miss it. That is my job too as the teacher.

The apostle Paul, in his teaching met real-life need after need. He taught on: love, marriage, divorce, pain, suffering, hardship, anxiety, grief, joy, peace, contentment, anger, factions, immorality, lawsuits, gossip, attitudes, fornication, weakness, rebuke, restoration, gluttony, drunkenness, lewdness, rudeness, deceit, patience, and scores of other life areas.

In your classroom with your age-group, do you know their needs? In this day and the sins of our society, some of your students may be caught up in a variety of "secret" sins. Whether it be lying, cheating, stealing, drugs, social drinking, MTV, pornography, an affair, gossip, dating the unsaved, or a myriad of other sins.

Let me challenge you to read the book *Already Gone* by Ken Ham and Britt

Beemer. It is a very factual book study of fundamental churches like yours and mine. The study concerns those in their twenties, who used to be in church each Sunday, but now are disengaged, with no intent to return.

"We are losing many more people by middle school and many more by high school than we will ever lose in college. . . They were lost while still in the fold. They were disengaging while they were still sitting in the pews. They were preparing their exit while they were faithfully attending youth groups and Sunday Schools. . . Students didn't begin doubting in college, they simply departed by college."

They found that **61%** who used to be a regular member of a church like yours are now "spiritually disengaged." This study did not include what we would consider liberal churches. Let us face it, this is what we are producing in our fundamental churches, up to 61%. They cannot defend their faith when the doubtful world of unbelievers is laid side-by-side. You need to read this book.

Our teaching must strike home where our students live. The more we can discern needs and meet those needs through passionate teaching, the Lord is always there to help us to creatively reach their heart.

Why am I teaching this lesson? What would be the ideal outcome? What is the ultimate destination on this journey?

A Review Of Key Thoughts:

1. Content is a goal, but not the higher goal. What is that higher goal of teaching?

_____-_____

2. Change can take place in your Sunday School class, before you dismiss, but not without the O_____.

3. Name a few things that can grab the attention of children, teens, or adults while you are teaching (take your pick): (1) _____

_____

(2)_____(3)_____

4. In your mind, describe how you could set up a "Situation Room" in your class, and for what is the purpose? _____

_____

_____

Chapter EIGHT

Methods, Techniques, And Classroom Involvement!

Methods, techniques, and classroom involvement are major for teachers. They compliment the Word of God, but never replace the reading, illustrating, searching, and explaining verse by verse. This chapter is not exhausting all methods and techniques known, for they fill books and more books. Our goal is to be knowledgeable of those that work best for us and to use them at appropriate times. Methods help us to care for different students who have their own or best methods of learning. It is a visual for one, a role-play for two others, and it is repetition for several others.

We must acknowledge that people have favorite learning styles that help them to grasp and to retain much better than other ways. This is a major flaw in teachers who refuse to read or never strive to solve their classroom problems. Some have no clue that half or more of the class learn through visuals as their best style of learning, yet they have used no visuals for years. That is sad. However, the better teacher develops his skills well in order to use the various learning styles of different students.

When it is words and words and that is all for everyone, some will not "get it," no matter how good you think you are.

VIII. Methods, Techniques, And Classroom Involvement

1. Active, Not Passive, But Under Control

2. What Is Interactive Learning?

3. Getting Kids to Listen Intently!

4. Getting More Than A "Grunt" Out Of Teens!

5. Getting Adults to Wake Up More Often!

6. Enthusiasm Is An Attitude!

7. Enthusiasm Is An Action!

8. Classroom Spirit- Dress Up The Place!

9. Developing Spirit Within The Student!

10. Developing Creativity For The Ministry!

11. The Discipline Of Children (The Positive Approach)!

Let Us First Give A Reminder Of How Jesus Taught, Our Teacher Of All Teachers!

Think for a moment between the methods and techniques of Jesus and what we have available today.

Whereas today we have all the values of the technical gadgets such as colorful marker boards, overhead projectors, power point, brilliant flannel-graph and poster boards; Jesus had none of those. His classroom could be set up in a moment of time. His classroom was portable, along a sea shore, a hillside, or among the vines and branches.

Yes, Jesus used the more formal synagogue, but when the students left for home, the teacher left on a field trip to the streets and paths where those same students lived for the next six days. The classroom became the living rooms, the play grounds, the fish factories, the orchards, or the wells of water. The pool of Bethesda was one, the wedding of Cana another, and the multitudes of pathways throughout the countryside. I would think that the ten lepers were happy to see a "circuit-walking" teacher come close enough to where they lived for another lesson!

The teacher taught truth in relation to real life. But then, as the example, He demonstrated and role-played the truth before their very eyes! Ah, Lord God, that we might be like you!

The Son of God never sat down with His disciples (as far as we know) and taught them principles of teaching, but we find that He taught everywhere. As He dealt with a person one-to-one, with crowds, Jesus was saying to us, "do it this way."

One of the most revealing verses that I heard many years ago was when Jesus walked along the real life trails, gazed into Heaven and said, "For I do always those things that please him" (John 8:29b). What a powerful reminder for us to use as our "thought of the day" for the next twenty-five years! In other words, He is teaching us that our words and actions should both glorify

God. He was without sin, and so were His actions! He was teaching us that the godly walk on this earth needs to line up with what we teach or preach. He was God in both. So, our goal is emptiness of self and to be filled with the Spirit of God! It is an everyday emptiness and an everyday filling. Wow!

Take a simple look at a passage and see how Jesus teaches us, and at the same time He teaches us how to teach!

The Parable Of The Good Samaritan

(Luke 10:25-37)

1. Introduction vss. 25-28 (There is my introduction to the lesson)

2. Reason To Listen vs. 29 (There is my "attention getter")

3. Illustration vss. 30-32 (compare to a modern similarity)

4. Truth to Live By vss. 33-35 ("need seen, assignment given")

5. Apply vs. 36 (consider, think, ponder, discuss, and bring to a decision)

6. Practice vs. 37 (Here is my response time back to God)

Although Jesus did not say, "Now all you teachers out there, this is how you teach;" but actually He did! His Book is overwhelmingly full of perfect examples of teaching. We find that as we read and study!

Jesus taught everyone at every opportunity: the leper, the lame, the blind, the lunatic, the poor, the Pharisees, the old, and the children. Name your problem, Jesus was there. The people saw His passion and His compassion!

In my personal *study Bible* there are **432** things listed that Jesus taught on, and a study Bible is certainly not an exhaustive list.

*There are listed over 80 prayers and what they teach us.

*37 miracles and the lesson of each.

*39 parables and the lesson in each.

*55 events in the Galilean ministry of Jesus and His teaching on that occasion.

*42 events of Jesus in His Judgment and Perean ministry.

*Jesus' final week at Jerusalem lists 45 events and the teaching played out there.

*The Resurrection through the Ascension listed 12 events.

*Think of all the prophesies of the Messiah and fulfilled in Jesus Christ.

Again, my favorite author on teaching, **Howard Hendricks** reminds us that "Jesus employed a variety of creative methods such as **overstatement** (Mark 5:29-30); **proverb** (6:4); **paradox** (12:41-44); **irony** (Matt. 16:2-3); **hyperbole** (23:23-24); **riddle** (11:12); **simile** (Luke 13:34); **pun** (Matt. 16:18); **allusion** (John 2:19); and **metaphor** (Luke 13:32)."

In the wonderful book of **Psalms**, every chapter is God teaching us. Take a tour sometime and refresh your mind as to the enormous amount of life-related issues He covers. For example:

In Psalm 1 He teaches us: The righteous/ the ungodly

In Psalm 3 He teaches us: To see victory when facing defeat.

In Psalm 4 He teaches us: The Lord will hear when I call.

In Psalm 5 He teaches us: In the morning will I direct my prayer unto thee.

In Psalm 6 He teaches us: The Lord will receive my prayer.

In Psalm 7 He teaches us: God judges the righteous, is angry at the wicked.

In Psalm 8 He teaches us: What is man, that thou art mindful of him?

In Psalm 15 He teaches us: Characteristics of the godly.

In Psalm 19 He teaches us: The heavens declare the glory of God.

In Psalm 21 He teaches us: Trust in the Lord and be not afraid.

150 Psalms teach us in almost every verse what we need to know about our God!

In *Psalm 119* the Lord reminds us in 176 verses on the value of His Word!

Solomon spoke 3,000 proverbs and 1,005 songs. At least 800 are listed in the book of *Proverbs.* There is where we find wisdom and knowledge and understanding!

From the *all-inclusive first verse* of the Bible, to the *all-concluding* last verse of our Bible He teaches us!

Thank you, dear Lord, for being our **Teacher** of all teachers!

VIII. Methods, Techniques, And Classroom Involvement

1. Active, Not Passive, But Under Control

To be passive is to sit by and watch something happen without having a word to say or any part, even as much as a touch. That is not always bad and sometimes a necessity, but when the lesson is desired to be understood, to be thoroughly grasped, and to learn, then the passive approach for students is the incorrect approach. It has its place, but when learning is supposed to be the outcome, it must be heavy on the active side, not passive.

It begins when the teacher allows time for interaction. Without it planned into the teaching time slot, the teacher will probably not allow it, and certainly not encourage it.

But wait a minute, that is how students learn best! When students sit there and do nothing, see nothing, say nothing, write nothing, and go home with nothing, little is retained.

It begins when the teacher allows time for interaction.

A teacher may say, "But I have taught that way for twenty years." The solution is to change. Change over time, but start now and consistently add involvement in future lessons. Variety greatly helps students, while being very predictable leads to yawning, stretching, and falling out of chairs.

For starters, use some of these: (1) Ask 2-3 questions as you teach (2) Try a short discussion (3) Supply a half-page take home note sheet (4) Use a whiteboard as you brainstorm for quick short answers (5) Read Scriptures as a class (6) Assign some students to review at each ten-minute interval of the lesson (7) Raise a problem to solve as students give possible answers (8) From sixth grade and above the long-used buzz group will help (9) As a group, can we quote a verse together, or a series of "class verses" to begin the lesson time? (10) Can we review the last three class lessons, using the verse and objective of each?

The idea here is simply to try an idea, not all on the same day, but could you try one idea a week for the next ten weeks? Slowly, consistently, you add two per week and keep giving a positive reminder for students to be a part of class.

2. What Is Interactive Learning?

In its simplest form it is to maximize involvement in the lesson time, to interact with what is said or shown. The teacher is still in control, but guides others to get in on the "real life" part of understanding. The teacher is in control, but welcomes all to get in on the process.

"Interaction is like a baited hook. It attracts attention, engages, 'hooks' and draws people into the message that is being communicated." *Lynn Wilford Scarborough* in **Talk Like Jesus.**

A classroom discussion does not have to take all of your "talking time." You can have a one-minute, two or three minute discussion, then back to your point. It is like a breath of fresh air from long periods of lecture. You are always in charge. Use shorter periods of time, it will help you to get into and out of discussions.

For some teachers this may be an unfamiliar approach, that of allowing a student to add a comment or ask a question. Most teachers I have known in these forty years are not against some inter-action, it is just that they were not taught that way growing up. Some may feel unskilled to handle such unexpected questions or comments.

Most of their former teachers just started talking and did not end until the bell rang. A multitude of today's teachers were for years taught that Sunday School is where you sit and listen. And so, they have been sitting and listening since about the sixth grade.

The classroom of today must come alive and must be relevant to the issues of the day. Students cannot just sit through their years of church with unanswered questions and no opportunity to ask them and no teacher who will allow time for questions. Our Bible studies are not just to teach what we must know, but why we need it, and how it works in real life. You cannot do that effectively without involvement.

I often hear preachers blast the art of drama, because they have seen it abused with high emotion, dancing, and other extremes. They wipe out the whole art with a blanket statement. Yet, short dramatic Biblical presentations help many to be a part, to see the truth acted out, to feel it, and to remember it for years to come!

In the book by Nicky Chavers, *The Value of Biblical Drama*, he states, "The whole Bible is dramatic. It is the most dramatic book in the world. . .Can you hear the voice of God calling, 'Adam! Adam! Where art thou?' Can you feel the shame of the man and woman as God sees them hiding themselves among the trees and calls once more, 'Adam!' 'I have heard thy voice in the garden,' Adam says, 'And I was afraid. I was afraid because I was naked and

I hid myself."'

Think of the dramatic scenes, if reenacted in a short 4-5 minute story or drama, students could get the full impact of the hour: The creation of all things; the creation of man and woman; temptation and sin; tower of Babel; Noah and the ark; the birth and life and death and resurrection of Christ; the miracles of Jesus; and hundreds more. The whole Bible is a drama!

Teacher, **you** must learn. You say I just do not know how to relate. Read. Read some more. Find out how to get those teens to open up. In a large study done in the book *Already Gone* by **Ken Ham & Britt Beemer**, they tell it like it is. It was a study of church drop-outs, now in their twenties, from churches just like yours, who have no intentions of returning. Here is just one quote:

"Almost 90 percent of them were lost in middle school and high school. By the time they got to college they were already gone! About 40 percent are leaving the Church during the elementary and middle school years! Most people assumed that elementary and middle school is a fairly neutral environment where children toe the line and follow in the footsteps of their parents' spirituality. Not so. I believe that over half of these kids were lost before we got them into high school."

3. Getting Kids To Listen Intently

Impossible? That may have been your initial thought after reading the title of this section. I would partially agree. However, the thought here is to provide for "spurts of intensity," not long 15-30 minutes of intensive listening.

The Hurried Child, by David Elkind reminds us to be careful with the children: "Children are most like us in feeling, least like us in thinking."

At the end of this chapter, you will see a "positive" approach to the discipline or control of kids over a long Sunday School hour or even longer Children's Church,

VBS, Kids Rally, or such. You will see how using "spurts" of time is what children can handle. They can go for 5-7 minutes of really listening intently, quoting verses, reading together, reviewing together, doing a word study, etc., being intense, then easing the pressure. This can happen several times in short blasts, but not long times.

> *"Children are most like us in feeling, least like us in thinking."* D. Elkind

In the book *Reach Every One You Teach* by Englebretson/LeFever, we read, "Preschoolers: Is it any wonder that preschoolers ask *Why?* so much? Their brains are hungry for input from a variety of sources – and you're one of them! Preschoolers are: (1) questioners; (2) able to focus on only one aspect of a situation at a time; (3) sensory learners; (4) able to do many more things physically than toddlers and twos; (5) group learners; and (6) roaming learners."

For example, let us study our key verse for the next six minutes. We will define words, illustrate what it means in real life, then quote it 3-4 times. To make it intense, we lay out the reason for every child not to miss the truth: (1) Give a reason for listening. (2) Give a time-line or goal for really listening (4-5-6 minutes). (3) Promise a game at the end of 6 minutes (a game that reinforces your truth). (4) Remind "Hawkeyes" to watch for those who sit up the straightest, keep their hands in their lap, and no talking, unless they are supposed to. (5) Put the verse or action-words on a marker board for kids to see. (6) Role Play the verse, or act it out. (7) Remind students that the Bible Review Game will cover the next 6 minutes!

Note: All the above helps to keep the attention on the 5-6 minute period of time needed for intensity. These techniques will help to clarify it more in section 10 – The Discipline Of Children.

Go for the six minute intense learning, then ease the tension. In another ten minutes, do it again. Perhaps your next "intense teaching" time will be in story form.

Storytelling has been called *"the only painless form of learning."* It is so easy to listen to an interesting story. It is the most remembered part of the whole lesson.

Students can go home and tell the whole story over again. So, if you will insert the truth inside the story, they go home with both!

> *Storytelling: "The only painless form of learning."*

Take time to "master" the story. In the book by Grant and Reed, *Telling Stories To Touch The Heart,* we see some good help, "Mastery means you know what to do with your hands, eyes, and feet. In short, mastering the story means more than memorizing the words; it means controlling the body, the voice, and the emotions of the storyteller as well."

4. Getting More Than A "Grunt" Out Of Teens

In the excellent book **Creative Bible Teaching**, they list five "non-negotiable" guidelines of youth ministry effectiveness.

1. Youth learn best through direct experience.

2. Youth learn best from caring role models.

3. Youth learn best when they are active in discovering truth.

4. Youth learn best when a variety of methods are used.

5. Youth learn best when lessons are relevant and needs focused.

Looking back over my first twenty years of ministry with teens, I can see in each of the five above a multitude of illustrations. Highland Park Baptist in Chattanooga, at that time, had an active attendance that grew from 5,000 weekly to over 10,000 attending. Our teen group was large. In order to impact many at one time, we planned larger events. Some of our activities brought 1500 teens out of the woodwork. We went after groups of public school kids at the same time. Our Bible Clubs, held in neighborhood homes close to Jr. High and Sr. High locations, reached a high of one thousand teens a week in forty Clubs. You can start with one, then two, but start!

To teach our "regular" youth group to be involved and active, *they* were used to reach the other teens and especially to connect with their "own kind." The Great Commission – Matthew 28:19-20 is for all believers. Kids can reach kids, teens can reach children and teens, and adults can reach all ages.

As teen outreach reached a high of 160 teens weekly knocking on doors, lessons were developed to help them. Since teens have never been taught how to talk to children, we teach them. It is an ideal area for them to talk to someone who does not over-shadow them. It is another good avenue to allow them to be involved in the things of the Lord! Some of those lessons taught were (1) Respect the child for who he is; (2) Do not make kids feel stupid; (3) Their vocabulary is not as long as yours; (4) Their understanding of terms is not far along; (5) He has a name, and it is not "Hey, Kid;" (6) Children love teens, compliment them; (7) Slow down in your talk; (8)

Watch the child's eyes and facial/body features; (9) Keep it simple; (10) Ask questions, use questions to get started; (11) Let the decisions be theirs, not yours; (12) Avoid the 5 minute dilemma (that everyone has to be saved in five minutes or less). Then, we taught them many methods and techniques of dealing with children. You can see all the above developed fully in the book **Sharing Christ With Children.**

Teens need to be a part. Being a part of what is happening is where the best of learning takes place. It is doing and experiencing.

Our church took teens to the mission field for many years. The purpose was for real learning to take place. It was so they could see and recognize the real world. Help them to gain a world-view like no other. You should hear teens open up about missions and their concern for much poorer folks and little children. You do not have to start the conversation and beg them to say something, because they start it and they continue it all day long.

Action involvement always gets more than a "grunt" out of teenagers. Plan some special times for your teens: (1) In the S.S. lesson (2) In periodic church services (3) In High School Bible Clubs (4) In neighborhood outreach (5) In hosting an outreach to children (6) In VBS (7) In visiting a local nursing home with a planned agenda (8) Doing a VBS program for another area church that needs the help (9) In distribution of flyers to attract teens to your next activity (10) In tract blitzes (11) In fund raisers (12) In serving tables for adult banquets (13) In hosting a beautiful Valentine Banquet for kids. Get the idea?

Sign up a teen each week to give their personal testimony, or to introduce another teen to the whole group, or to provide a one-minute devotional, or to lead songs in Sunday School.

In your class, teens will respond well to visuals, good storytelling, something short to write down, buzz groups, listening teams, and other interactive involvement. The teacher who only talks from start to finish is in trouble. Whether he knows it or not, he needs to watch the body mannerisms of the students.

> *Teens open up when it is their turn to talk.*

Just start thinking. Teens open up when it is their turn to talk or to be "in the thick of things"!

From ***Why Nobody Learns Much Of Anything At Church*** by Thom and Joani Schultz, "Explaining a concept to someone else is usually more helpful to the explainer than the listener. So why not let the students do more teaching? That's one of the chief benefits of interactive learning. . . Interactive learning depends on students working together to make discoveries rather than teachers imparting all the facts and ideas."

5. Getting Adults To Wake Up More Often!

Over time and through much traveling you just about see it all. I have literally fallen asleep in adult classes, and I was not even sleepy. I have found myself wondering if I would ever see the teacher look at a person in the room, besides the ceiling. I have found myself starting to count the "Uhhh's" of the teacher. I have felt the effects of hypnosis after 150 taps of a pen on the podium. I have held my Bible straight up in front of my face as a teacher begins pronouncing Bible words or names to keep my laughs to small whimpers. I have stood at the end and by the time I reached the classroom door, I could not have possibly told you what the lesson was about. But these are the uncommon times.

A blaring observation is the lack of **connection** with the students and real life, and the lack of involvement. Although many adults have walked with God for 40-50-60 years, there is rarely an opportunity for them to speak or share real life experiences. They too need your help in opening up some avenues of involvement.

(1) Adults often fear failure in front of their peers. The teacher must find areas where that risk is minimized.

(2) Adults do have a thirst to learn. Life-long learning is a growing attitude among adults who have had the taste of knowledge before. They often have personal selections of the ways they would choose to learn. Many enjoy the avenue of reading, while others prefer the TV (travel, how it is made, history, biographies, life styles, and even the old shows (Andy and Barney, Ole' Yeller, etc.). Others still travel often. The Learning Channel is widely seen by the adult age group.

(3) Adults can be drawn in to learn. Most authors mention three areas which motivate adults to learn: Pleasure-Need-Knowledge. Give them an interesting topic and logical presentation and they will listen well.

> *Adults often have personal selections of the ways they would choose to learn.*

Problem solving is a most powerful way to engage the adult mind, and the groundwork can be laid through at-home preparation by some adults. In other words, they plan how they will respond to a key question. They have a week to prepare their answer. Problem solving causes students to think – to sort out – to draw a conclusion. Adults love to give their opinions.

(4) Offer diversity as your schedule for the weeks ahead. Your class is many parts of the whole body of Christ. The needs are many, as they come with much baggage, unknown problems from the past forty years or more. But that helps the whole group to see the truth in their own scenario. Application cannot touch all people from only one illustration or method.

Adults are involved by such techniques as: Readings, Projects, Surveys, Questions, Problem-Solving, Written Assignments, Group Work Projects, Listening Teams, Buzz Groups, along with lively and meaningful lecture from God's Word!

Something To Read About:
(1) Read the key passage several times. (2) Read parallel Scriptural passages. (3) Read to prepare a one-minute answer. (4) Read to answer the Who, What, When, Where, etc. (5) Read to answer assigned questions.

Find The Answers:
(1) Give four or five questions to find answers to share next week. (2) Relate a few questions that ask for real life scenarios. (3) Prepare three questions to use in review.

You Are The Teacher:
(1) In which verse of the passage applies to where you work or worked? (2) Give students a "What if this happened to you. . ." situation to answer in class. (3) Give a scenario that could have multiple right answers. (4) List one or more problems at work and the best way to solve the ordeal. (5) Give a

probable home situation that could occur as a result of practicing this verse at home.

Teacher Thoughts: Plan Ahead To Add Involvement:
(1) Add in two short discussion questions or situations of life. (2) Can you highlight with a red marker your lesson subject that is seen in your local newspaper? (3) Take one term to be discussed in the first five-minutes of class, such as: substitution, redeemed, rapture, surrender of life, etc. For the next ten weeks, define and illustrate a Bible word that applies to real life, and review each one each week, then move into your current lesson. (4) Recall a personal illustration that matches the truth for this week. (5) Paraphrase this verse as though you are helping the students to understand it.

In the book ***You Can Teach With Success,*** by David Schantz he speaks of identifying a boring class: "Heads begin to tilt and bodies sag into the pews. Spiders begin weaving webs between students. A middle aged man opens his billfold and begins to clean and sort its contents on the pew beside him. An attractive lady borrows a pocket knife and begins to do her manicure, and a crude man next to her is practicing covert nasal explorations."

In the book ***Creative Bible Teaching*** by Richards and Bredfeldt, they list 72 ideas for getting adults involved in these type of categories: (1) Questions (2) Readings (3) Projects (4) Interviews and surveys (5) Problem Solving (6) Written Assignments (7) Group Work. You need this book!

"Don't assume anything when it comes to application of truth in life. Our lesson goal is not if each student leaves knowing only a memory verse or central thought of a Bible text. Each must also know something specific God wants him to do as a result of exposure to His Word." From the book ***How***

To Be The Best Sunday School Teacher You Can Be by Terry Hall.

6. Enthusiasm Is An Attitude!

I choose to be enthusiastic. I choose to develop a better spirit of enthusiasm.

> *"Don't assume anything when it comes to application of truth to life." T. Hall*

1. Remind yourself of the power of enthusiasm.

It is "catching." If you teach **children,** just learn to latch onto their enthusiasm. If you teach **teens**, remember this is one of the last "shots" you have to show your spirit for Christ and the Church. If you teach the **adults,** counteract the tendency to slow down the thrill of it all, but keep the thrill like you had when salvation was new!

You are developing the attitude you have now into the minds of your students (a scary thought). The church teacher or the school teacher is planting "seed thoughts" in the minds of children about their future careers. You have influence!

When we first moved to Milford, Ohio our second son had little idea of the career he would pursue someday. As a 10th grader nothing was clear. For the next two years he was under his church teacher who was also a policeman. His testimony of being a Christian and still being an officer was very satisfying to my son. No where else in our family did he get that influence, but he did in church. Upon graduation his mind was fixed. The first few years were spent in the same police department that his teacher was in. Now, he is a fine detective, and will use his influence along the way.

2. *The thrill of ministry is that you never know who you are talking to.*

No matter what season of life, you have influence. *A teacher creates influence!* Whatever the age, people can change when they come into contact with a change agent. That should be you.

In the thought-provoking book ***Influencer***, by a group of authors have surveyed the world for years, finding those often unknown people who have become change-agents for the good. In this quote they show us a problem of how many workers in a field can actually give-up on change and settle for living with the problem: "Of the speeches, classes, and activities that took place at that conference (16th International AIDS Conf.), over *90 percent* dealt with how to cope with the effects of AIDS. . . less than *10 percent* of the speeches at the conference even speculated on how to change the behavior that drives the disease in the first place. Here we have a disease that would never infect another human being if people simply thought and behaved differently."

A teacher creates influence.

The preacher that knocked on my door had no idea that within less than five minutes I would be on my knees and for forty plus years later would still be serving the Lord, even in a fulltime manner. Since I had never met the man, his influence did little for the moment, but his presence helped me to take that step of commitment that I had not taken before. That one "touch" by a man of God has carried me for a long way! He did not know my need *until he asked*.

3. *This is your "spot"* and your time to show what a Christ-centered life is all about. Adult teachers should pour their heart into adults. Some have quit serving and yet the door is still wide open for them to return. You can still encourage those who are physically challenged today to learn the great power of prayer.

4. A teacher sees potential when none can be seen!

On one blue sky day flying to the West Coast, I crossed an advertisement in a magazine. I think it was trying to grab my attention for the latest new car on the market. I read words similar to these below, and immediately my mind raced to children. I changed the ad around to say this: *The potential in a child is often unnoticed, undeveloped, and unused. That is tragic. Because when the potential of a child is never developed, a terrible thing happens:* **NOTHING!**

Yet, God has gifted all with one or more gifts that could be used to bring Him glory throughout life. God uses people (teachers especially) to develop that potential. That motivates me! Remember, role-modeling is called the greatest unconscious form of learning. A teacher creates that influence.

So, how is your attitude?

7. Enthusiasm Is An Action!

1. Enthusiasm is felt, seen, heard, and remembered for years to come.

Think for just a moment and you will probably remember a teacher's name that would bring joy to your face, and probably enthusiasm was a reason you remember that name.

Personally, I like to use a "pep talk of self talk" before I teach. If you have not tried it yet, be my guest. Grade yourself after your next session is over. If you would give yourself an "A," then award yourself a snickers bar, or some other "high-end" award!

2. *The prepared teacher explodes with confidence.* Confidence brings enthusiasm! You do not face that class wishing it was over, but wishing it would hurry up and begin. The effort it takes for being prepared brings great benefits, with confidence being one of the best.

Action results from mastering the lesson. You are ready. Instead of eight pages

> *Confidence brings enthusiasm!*

of notes, you arrive at class with ½ page of reminders. You have just key words that remind you of what you have already mastered. There is much action in the classroom and the teacher is free to express himself with eye-contact, jesters, and close-encounters with the student.

Enthusiasm in the classroom does not mean you have to do cart-wheels, flips, and flops. Enthusiasm hits all of the emotional levels as we communicate. When you are yourself, you can smile, laugh, cry, be serious, be calm, frown with the rest of your total body following suit, all within one lesson's time.

Spend some time in front of a large mirror as you practice what you plan to say. You will see the good expressions, and those that did not compliment the words you just said at all. It will help you in your enthusiastic expressions.

8. Classroom Spirit- Dress Up The Place!

The dictionary takes two words to define the one word "spirit." It is made up of both enthusiasm and loyalty.

Enthusiastic does not necessarily mean cartwheels, flips, and extremely loud screams. That is a way of expression that enthusiastic feeling or spirit that is on the inside. But, there are milder ways to show spirit!

But, spirit pairs the two: **Enthusiasm and loyalty.** It is one thing to express a lively spirit of enthusiasm for the team, the event, or the person, and then go out later to express a disloyalty toward what you cheered earlier. It takes both!

1. It begins with the Leader's spirit.

You have heard the term, "if momma ain't happy, nobody's happy." It is the same in every classroom, every teacher to student environment. If the leader of the pact is not happy and positive and enthusiastic, nobody is. Enthusiasm is taught, and it is caught!

2. Classroom spirit can be cultivated.

Even the right kind of spirit can be developed.

Write out your #1 dream for your class this year. If you had the best class success ever by the end of this year, what would that be? In your own words, what is your ideal #1 dream? Understand that you will never achieve a #1 dream for a class without a #1 team pursuing that dream. Therefore, I probably need to develop an excellent **team** spirit. Let us start with your #1 dream. *Spend a little time now!*

Once my dream is in my mind and now on paper, including the steps it will take to get there, there is another plan I need. To create a class-team-spirit, what must improve or change from what I did last year? Again, write it down.

What else contributes to class spirit? *Your physical classroom is a part.*

3. Does the room teach?

What grabs the attention during those non-teaching moments? What is it, if seen repetitively for the next six weeks would remain fixed in young minds for months to come? If not anything is in place, why not? If not, when?

(a) Review keeps truth fresh in young minds.
Why should that great truth or that key statement you gave last week never be reviewed again? Whatever you want remembered long-term you had better say it more than once. Review and repetition are two key words that are a teacher's best friend.

> *Review and repetition are two key words that are a teacher's best friend.*

(b) Is your classroom colorful?
Children are raised in a very colorful world. Age-appropriate colors should fill the room! If it is dull, paint it. Wallpaper it in jellybeans! Do something besides wishing it was more colorful.

The **Lockfast** material from *Master Ministries* is a colorful and versatile covering for display boards. Not creative? Ask someone who can help. Buy an easel. Make your list to change your classroom environment. My classroom needs:

(1) _____ (2) _____ (3) _____

"Visuals greatly enhance the effectiveness of your teaching. A visual, properly used, will grab the students' attention, help him understand the lesson, and cause him to remember it. Why would anyone teach without them?" *I Can't*

Wait Till Sunday Morning! by Ed Dunlop.

(c) Is your classroom organized?

Plastic file boxes neatly store classroom odds 'n ends. Handouts, news-notes, etc. arranged orderly for students give the feeling of anticipation. Are you organized? Are your notes ready? Are your visuals in order? Is your marker board clean and ready with markers that actually work? Your tools must be ready to go.

What poster would appeal to **children**? You will find a world of posters on character and even Bible pictures in a School Supply Store. What would appeal and teach for **teens**? How about the **adult** classroom? **Rose Publication** is an excellent source for adult posters and teaching tools. See them on line.

(d) Is your classroom out of date?

Are Christmas decorations still up in March? Shame, Shame! Even good posters can over-stay their welcome. Does everything look old?

(e) Is your classroom clean?

I know, I should not have asked the question. There is no excuse for a dirty un-kept room. Would your room be best described as a flea market? A cluttered room gives only negative reactions.

Now, let us go from the physical classroom, to the very **physical student.**

9. Developing Spirit Within The Student

(a) What spiritual goals are set?

None? Then expect the least spiritual results. If we can set goals for many other areas of life for all the ages of life, why should spiritual goals be any less intense? We plan and detail our objectives based on each individual person. We view man as made in the image of God! What will you do this year to find the needs of your students and to address them in your teaching or counsel? *You need to know, and you will never know for sure unless you ask.*

Teachers cannot spend their year assuming that each child, teen, or even adult are secure in their salvation. Never assume a church-child or teen is saved because of "whose home" he comes from.

(b) Other than the person's name, what do you know about him?
Do you know what "kind of" home he comes from? As a child, there is usually a reason why the child acts the way he acts, and the home is the number one suspect. You need to know that. Have you met his parents? What are his interests? The more I know about who I teach, the better teacher I become. With adults, it would help you to know your students' backgrounds, without getting into all the baggage. However, every little bit helps. It will help you to prepare your lesson when it comes to application, illustrations, and the things "that hit home" in a lesson. What are his interests, hobbies, strengths, and skills?

(c) Always encourage your students!
Whatever you can find to say a positive word about, make a note in order to not forget. Send encouraging note cards to all age groups of students. You are helping your own cause for the times you will need to teach in some "touchy" areas of life.

For adult ministries, I have noticed over the years that good pastors are always there in the big times of life: births, operations, crisis, marriages, or death. Why? These are the opportunities to minister and to establish your love and concern for the whole family. Your rapport with your students just went up another notch.

> *Refuse to pray the "casual way."*

(d) Pray by name and by need for your students. Refuse to pray the casual way, "Lord, bless my class next week," end of prayer. Sometimes we are too general in our prayers. No names, no needs, just "bless 'em all, dear Lord, bless 'em all." Refuse to take the "quickie-get-it-out-of-the-way" route. The more you pray by name and by need the better teacher you become!

"An effective way to praise is to praise what the person did, rather than the person, and then encourage the person to do the achievement or deed again. The technique is called specific praise. . .The reason people are most likely to do well again is that they know that you saw them do something specific." *The First Days of School* by Harry and Rosemary Wong.

10. Developing Creativity For The Ministry!

Developing your own creativity is a long-term mind set for those who will "head the pack." It is not that the burden falls totally upon your shoulders, and everyone else just waits until that great idea drips from your lips. **Others** must be led to be a part of the process, whether that mind-set is in place yet or not. The business, school, or church **without the all-contributing "team"** will always be in for a long, slow growth process.

Creativity can be as simple as taking an existing idea and questioning yourself: What if I doubled it, shortened it, and expanded the number involved? What if I did it every day, once a month? What if it was bigger, louder, brighter, or more portable? Questions bring the creativity for many people!

Good ideas come when you think. When you refuse to take time to think, nothing comes out. Thinking generates more thinking, and that is where the ideas come from. Becoming a good thinker is not complicated. It is a discipline that we can learn, but demands self-discipline to set yourself up in a think time. We have mentioned a "think time" in another chapter. This is the practice that changed my life for the good!

Walt Disney said, "It's always fun to do the impossible." Again, he said, "Impossible dreams don't know they're impossible."

The people in your life impact your thinking.

The people in your life impact your thinking. Find people who will stretch you. *(Take them out to eat – I'm available almost anytime!)*

The idea *generator* is the one we call creative. Jack Welch, longtime CEO for GE said, "The hero is the one with the ideas." But, without a team of *implementers* every man comes to his level of incompetence.

Peter Drucker, management guru, said, "Abandoning the obsolete, the irrelevant, or the program with promise that never materialized is the key to innovation."

Learning To Innovate

You will find that occasionally you will come up with a new idea, almost as if you are the first person in history to think of it. But, more often than not your "new" idea was thought of hundreds of years ago. But that is alright. Just the thought time brought that idea out and with a bit of adjustment it could work "like" a new idea. Albert Einstein said, *"Imagination is more important than knowledge."*

Creativity is a thinking process, where there are no boundaries to rapid thoughts, such as in brainstorming. Let the thoughts flow, many of them. Later, you can "weed out" all the ideas until the best ones are left. From ten ideas, bring it down to five, then three, then choose the best one and "go with it." If it falters, you still have three or four other ideas.

Sometimes you win; sometimes the idea does not pan out. Sometimes you sink, and sometimes you swim. Even then, **sinking will make you want to swim all the more!**

One of the best books you can add to your reading library is b
y John Maxwell, entitled *Thinking For A Change*. It is a most excellent book that you will read over and over. Few books do I read multiple times, but this is one!

On page 114, he states, **"Seldom do I have an original idea. Often I take an idea that someone else gives me and raise it to a higher level. That has been my approach to creativity."**

Sometimes you sink, and sometimes you swim.

What an honest confession, but what great wisdom for us to grab onto early in life. That means that creativity is not just waiting for that lightening bolt to spell out an idea in words in the sky. We can look at existing materials or ideas or the techniques and see how to do them better, or to improvise for our particular business or ministry. It is exhilarating to gain a positive thought that seems good on the surface. It gives you that shot of energy to start!

"Einstein was once asked what the difference was between him and the average person. He said that if you asked the average person to find a needle in a haystack, she would stop when she found a needle. He, on the other hand, would tear through the entire haystack looking for all possible needles." *What A Great Idea! 2.0* by Chic Thompson

Never give up the thinking process. Whenever I have looked for an answer, if I just kept looking it always brings more and better ideas. It should become how we always approach the search for the best idea.

For example, the idea of having a teenage ministry at church is not new, almost all churches have one. But how can we enlarge such a ministry?

For a foundation, the church must realize that if they want a strong teenage ministry, your pre-teen ministry (children) must be exceptional. So, what is the difference from one church to another? The difference is leadership and the children's budget. It is not uncommon for Baptist churches to plan no more than 1% of the total church budget for a children's ministry. They just do not see it. They do not see the value of the child. They may say they do, but look at the budget. Many workers have to go to beg pastor for $30 every time they try to do something to reach children. That is not belief, it is disbelief. They do not see the church as a place needed to raise the next generation. They will agree with that, but deny it in the budget.

Children learn more in the childhood years than in the next 50-60 years to come. Yet, some still do not see it. Although in the largest surveys taken, 85% of all people who get saved are saved in our churches by the ages of 4-14. Yet, the evangelistic dollar spent on our churches sets only 20% aside for children or teen evangelism, yet 85% of the results come from the children and teens. Make sense of that! Yet, those who control the budget still do not see it. I have personally been there for too long.

So, back to my original thought: How do we enlarge our teenage ministry? When stagnant growth becomes the norm, go to your creative think time. Think outside the box of your church property. That is where the kids are anyway. How about starting a Bible Club for teens near a Jr. or Sr. High School using a Christian home nearby as the location. Once the first begins reaching kids, the second club brings the enthusiasm for another team of workers.

What has that got to do with teaching? Growth brings more teens to teach God's Word! More teens to be saved, more teachers to have a spot to teach and disciple and to fulfill God's Great Commission! There is no need for another teacher if there is no one to teach.

Leadership trains teachers and opens opportunities for ministry. Creativity sees something that is missing, finds an idea to fill it, but that is not the end. Creativity finds a way to expand a good idea. Continually pursuing an original idea allows you to innovate or to raise the original idea to a higher level. The idea expanded into forty Bible Clubs throughout Chattanooga, with a high of 1000 teens a week attending. Activities had teens coming for fun and the Gospel.

Now, let us expand again from our church to the neighborhoods, then into our schools. Getting a speaker into a high school assembly in a unique way promoted a church event that brought 7000 teens out for a Gospel message. They crammed into our 6000 seat auditorium.

Why did it work so well? Because one idea led to another, to another, and to another. Thinking brings to you innovating ways to win bigger wins! Imagine four, then six, then eight clubs full of teens. Is that not your ministry? Sure it is, so never stop thinking! Stop limiting your possibilities, for there are more just around the corner! However, unless someone takes the idea and runs with it, it dies.

Some Guidelines To Becoming Creative

1. **Learn the process of selecting several options** for most projects you wish to begin. There are probably more options than the first one you think of. There is usually not just one answer to your problem. I have literally had hundreds of times when this happened over the years. Once you think of your first way to make it happen, there is probably a better one just around the corner. Put them all down, without final judgment, then go back and make your #1 choice.

Philosopher Emile Chartier said, "Nothing is more dangerous than an idea when it's the only one you have."

2. **Brainstorm all of your workers.** They have the ability to think too. Maybe they have never spent any time thinking about your project. Some know the process, some will gradually catch on, but you will not know the quality of some to help you without giving them the opportunity. Brainstorming is a means of collecting thoughts, many thoughts on one subject. All of a sudden

you now have a resource of multiple possibilities!

When you desire the best ideas, go after a multitude of ideas, then pick from the best of many.

3. **Imagination is an absolutely wonderful word.** God has implanted into all of us the ability to imagine, to say "what if," or "what would happen if we did it this way?" **The more you imagine, the closer you are coming to that "best" solution.** Your role as the project manager is to spot that idea that feels good! See what would work. You will always have plenty of others who see only the problem.

> *Go after a multitude of ideas, then pick from the best of many.*

Former President Woodrow Wilson once said, **"I not only use all the brains that I have, but all that I can borrow."**

4. **Do not be afraid to fail.** Every failure should only make you better. Will you ever do that again? No. But, it does lead you to evaluate the failure, to see the process that brought it about, which, in turn will improve your thoughts for the solution. There are just too many variables or uncertainties for you to always be right the first time. Just the variable or people will cause many original directions to be changed or modified along the way.

5. **Always, always, evaluate your ministry.** One whole chapter of this book is dedicated to that process. Evaluation is a part of the creativity process too as you search for the "better way." Taking the time to evaluate will be a great investment to make on all of your projects. You are anticipating finding a better, faster, less costly, more effective solution. I love to stop, evaluate,

tweak, and move on! When I see how to "fix it" or improve my project that *pushes me!*

Practice being creative, until it becomes a habit for you to look at the same project, the methodology, the time involved in production, the cost, the options, and just wonder "what if." Are there new and better methods, new materials, short cuts, or less costly ways to get the same result?

While traveling, look at the billboards as each pass and evaluate on the basis of: Which one grabs your attention first? Are the words phrased the best? In five seconds can you understand what they are selling? How would you make it better, brighter, better worded? It simply makes you think. You look at it, evaluate it, improve it.

Coming up with options for any project is also being creative. Think of another way, which may open up a series of other ways. That is how it works, but without the effort to think I become one of those persons who just goes through life saying, "I'm not good at that." As we would say back in the hills, *Phooey! Baloney!* is another good word.

I carry with me a newspaper illustration when Delta was in deep trouble. The CEO at that time was listing his options to get this huge airline out of the pits and back on solid ground. He listed the option, then the risk of going that way:

Wait and see
"Fuel prices could fall and Delta could get the pension relief it seeks from Congress, allowing the crisis to abate."
The Risk

"Fuel markets are unstable; the Transportation Department has been silent on the airline crisis and what Congress might do is uncertain."

As he continued he listed six more scenarios:

Shed Assets. *The Risk.*

Get Smaller. *The Risk.*

Push the leverage button. *The Risk.*

Squeeze labor. *The Risk.*

Find a partner. *The Risk.*

Drop the big one (bankruptcy). *The Risk.*

That is the creative process. Let the ideas, the "what if" thoughts flow without questioning or debating at first. Find ten options, then take the time to evaluate each until the best two or three emerge.

When the business, the school, the church has thinkers available, problems will still arise, but not for long! Someone there is going to think their way out of the difficulty. Someone has to do something about it or it may go on for a very long time. There is another place where you can learn to *Push Yourself!*

Note for "11" below. *The next few pages deal specifically for those who teach children. If you prefer, skip over to chapter nine.*

11. The Discipline Of Children – *(The Positive Approach!)*

The first requirement of learning is to have their attention. If you do not have it, something else still does. However, keeping learners quiet often has nothing to do with actually teaching them. There must be control, but also involvement by students. You can have both!

Behavior may be more of an expression of a teacher problem than an actual kid problem. It may be that the teacher is the biggest problem of all.

The following notes are compiled from actual experience from the last forty years. My experience has included hundreds of children's sessions, from downtown big city kids, to ten junior boys in a classroom. This positive approach has lasted for all these years, and has worked every single time. The last large group included 600 bus kids, genuine good ole' bus children. It is great! Here are the details:

The Right Use Of Workers

Workers are to help control the children. Workers are not spectators, standing around the back talking. But, sometimes they have never been told what to do. Someone just told them to come over to Children's Church and it would help. They have no idea of how to help and nobody has told them how.

(1) One worker on his feet is worth two in the seat. I would much rather move a child than to sacrifice a worker by setting him in between two kids. If I had plenty of workers, that is fine, but most churches only have a few workers. I would be better off to move one of those kids and leave my worker free to roam.

(2) Workers should not block the view of children. Children should not have to lean on each other in order to see. It is a good idea to set up the chairs at least 6-8 inches apart and demand that they stay apart. This is a positive way to keep kids from bumping elbows from the start.

Key workers should face the children. Call them "Hawkeyes."

(3) Create a positive reason to watch the children. "Hawkeyes" look for good behavior, not bad. It is usually the exact opposite that we do. We set up a "Christian Bouncer" is what we do. Everybody knows that he is there for one reason- to find the meanest kid he can, as soon as possible, and toss him out. It is like ringing the bell for Round 1. Here we go again, put up your "dukes," it is time for Children's Church!

But, with Hawkeyes, your workers are not bad guys, they are now good guys looking for good behavior, not bad. As soon as they spot it in any child, the child will be picked to play the neat Bible games and win any prizes we have.

(4) Explain to the children every week why you have Hawkeyes. There are three basic rules that are always the same and are always repeated every week without fail: (a) Sit up straight (b) Keep your hands to yourself (c) No talking, unless you are supposed to talk.

Remember, these are kids, and there must be some time for them to release. They can sing, answer questions, play the review game, etc., but then there are times when they do not talk. They must understand these times clearly.

Hawkeyes stand to the side with a good view of each child. The Hawkeyes do not watch what goes on at the front, for the kids then know that they are not really watching them. As often as the director allows the Hawkeyes, pick out so many children who have been obeying the above rules to come play the games and win the prizes.

Remind kids of the rules every week.

The teacher will remind kids of the rules every week. Talk to the Hawkeyes back and forth as you are explaining what type of behavior to award, the children are hearing the rules over and over, at least 8-10 times at the beginning.

The Teacher: The teacher should never have to be the disciplinarian. The Hawkeyes are not going to leave their post to go correct misbehavior. So, who will? We will get to that in a bit!

(5) Once you begin with perfect attention, you really can maintain it throughout. If your Children's Church goes for an hour and one/half you obviously will not preach for that long, so what do you do? Our ministry has multiple games all ready to go. See our store at *masterclubs.org/store.*

In this section let us talk about the teacher and how he/she uses the Hawkeyes to help retain and then to regain attention throughout.

You can maintain the same amount of quiet throughout that you achieve in the beginning. What was that? Sitting up straight- Hands to yourself- No talking.

If you begin with perfect attention, you have a reference point to come back to when attention begins to lessen. What is that reference point? Sitting up straight- Hands to yourself- No talking. It is always the same. Kids can get use to your rules if they never change.

From here on the teacher/speaker operates on an attention span basis. When it wanders, bring it back again. When you see heads turning, body movement, yawning, stretching, etc., you are starting to lose attention. Do something to bring it back again to that reference point.

(6) Key points in maintaining attention.

(a) Bring in something new. Think it up right there in your story. For example: Boys, girls, you won't believe the next thing that happened. . .I am going to tell you as soon as you (1) Sit up straight (2) Keep your hands in your lap, and (3) No talking. Immediately they resume the posture and attention you started with at the beginning. The only thing that moves is their eyes, as they glance to see if the Hawkeye is watching. All I did was to remind them that the Hawkeye is watching. They keep forgetting that after a while.

(b) Bring in something suspenseful. Think up a suspenseful place in your story. Do as listed in (a) above.

It does not take a child very long at all to understand that the only way he is going to play those neat games and win those prizes is that he is picked by the Hawkeye, and the only way the Hawkeye is going to pick him is if he. . .

This technique is used throughout the whole time of Children's Church or any gathering of a large group of children. I may teach a Bible verse to the whole group for five minutes, then pick out so many Hawkeye winners to come play a game that may even reinforce the verse. Then, we go back to teaching again, for a few more minutes.

(c) Learn to watch for signs that you are losing control (heads turning, body movement, etc.). Do not allow it to deteriorate before regaining it.

(d) Make the quiet prize work for you. Small, inexpensive prizes become "tools" to help motivate good attention. The one used most often is small pieces of candy or small "doo-dads, gadgets, or gizmos." You simply cannot find giveaway items in a Bible Bookstore that are inexpensive. One rule is always the same: You cannot eat it or play with it. If you do, it is gone. Believe me, it is gone, that is the rule. They will obey your rules if you state them kindly and enforce them kindly.

(e) Make it attractive. A quiet prize is no good unless all the children want it! Wrap it up or select something colorful. Talk about how good it tastes.

(f) Make it mysterious. Keep them in suspense sometimes. Shake it, give hints, it really motivates the kids!

> *A quiet prize is no good unless all the children want it!*

Some final thoughts: Television has permanently altered the attention span of everyone, especially children. You must be creative in dealing with children.

Be positive. I would do exactly what I just told you if I had 600 "bus kids" in front of me, or if I had five junior boys in a class. There, I'd be my own Hawkeye.

The Major Problem Children

There are basically three types of problem children who disrupt and make effective teaching difficult. These are:

(1) The hostile child who is rebellious and angry and disobedient.
Some of our children are what we could call hostile children. The hostile child is usually very insecure and has a deep need to feel wanted. Many

children who are from broken homes or who have much parental rejection will develop hostility. They feel unwanted and because of this, anger builds up and they will vent it any way they can.

(2) The nuisance child who is not actively rebellious, but he continually does things to gain attention.

The things he does are always in the line of pestering someone, practical joking, etc. Many of this type go around and punch or bully others. This one usually comes from a background where there is a lack of attention and love. He craves attention, and being a nuisance is the only way he knows how to get it. Note: A proven principle of counseling is that a person would rather have negative attention than no attention at all. In other words, a child who is craving attention would rather be scolded or reprimanded for his actions (because this is still attention) than to have no attention at all.

(3) The clown child is also craving attention, so he uses clowning around.

He is the most easy to accept because his activities are not as annoying as the two preceding, but his problems are no less severe. He wants attention, and he can get it by being the class clown. He may make bird calls while you are teaching, throw paper airplanes, give a silly answer, or do just about anything for a laugh.

In summary, it should be clear that problem children are problems because they have a need in their life which must be met. They need to feel wanted or they need affection, and they try to get it in any way possible.

Train Your People To Discipline Alike

Other than your Hawkeyes (who do not look for problem children), use your other workers to stand around the perimeter of your room, casually looking for actual discipline problems.

Step 1. The Eye Contact

This is the first indication by you and to the child that "you know what he is doing and you do not like it." When he looks at you (and he will to see if you are looking at him), give a negative nod, the eyebrow, a frown, etc. We hope nobody saw us do that, but the child did, and he knows exactly what you said to him. This is done from a distance away.

Step 2. The Move Closer

If the problem continues, the worker should casually move closer to the problem child. Hopefully, still not drawing attention to the child, but he knows exactly why you have moved closer. In fact, we teach these informal workers to move around from time to time so the kids get used to it and do not necessarily expect anything.

Step 3. The "Voice" Of Discipline

If the problem child continues, the worker must now make the move to speak a word of warning in the child's ear. This should be done quickly, quietly, and with as little distraction as possible.

Step 4. Move the Child To The Back Of The Class

If the problem still exists, the child must be moved, quietly but swiftly to the rear.

Step 5. Move Child Outside The Door, But Can Still Hear

If the problem continues, move the child out of view of everyone, but where he can still hear. If this behavior is common, his parents must be confronted.

The Principle of Looking for Good Behavior, Not Bad!

1. Good Behavior Wins!
2. The Rules Have To Be Simple
3. The Rules have To Be Consistent
4. The Incentives Must Excite The Kids
5. The Involvement Games Must Be Fun
6. The "Hawkeyes" Must Be Fair
7. Misbehavior Cannot Continue

Explanation:

1. Good Behavior Wins!

That becomes your *major clue* for every week. Negative rules take a backseat to the positive approach. *Here is the "deal" you offer the children:*

"If I can spot you sitting up straight, hands to yourself, and no talking (unless you're allowed to be talking), then I am going to find you and pick you to come play our games and win our prizes. That is the deal!

This is what I say at least ten times every class we meet. This is my **deal** to them. They can understand very quickly that out of these boundaries there are no games to play, no prizes to leave with, and no recognition before others. It does

Avoid threatening over and over. .

not take long to understand that the rules are simple enough to pay the price in behavior to receive the benefits.

Your explanation, if given enthusiastically, will make the positive benefits so attractive that the negative is rarely mentioned.

Most teachers only threaten kids. *"If you do not stop that,"* or *"Next time you do that,"* or *"I've just about had it,"* these are the usual. But, here is the problem: You said the same thing ten minutes ago. They know that, **so your threats are no greater than anyone else's threats.** They hear that all week long. They know that adults do not carry through on their threats anyway.

The positive approach wins far more than the negative. You make the positive so attractive that they can not resist to obeying your simple rules!

2. The Rules Have To Be Simple

Often, with kids, the problem is there are no rules except those made on the spot and out of frustration. Your rules cannot be long or numerous. Rules must be *simple to understand and repeated "forever."* Every week, say it again from six to ten times. ***You cannot afford for them to forget the rules.***

"Boys and girls, today I will be looking for those who sit up the straightest, keep your hands to yourself, and no talking, unless you are supposed to talk..." It is a reminder to your regulars and to clarify the rules to new comers. Remember, the new ones have never heard your rules.

3. The Rules Have To Be Consistent

When you change the rules, it is frustrating. Some kids will just give up trying. *You must establish the value of your incentive to be worthy of obeying the rules to get it.*

Your rules must be consistently, yet lovingly ***enforced.*** For example, my rule on any award received is always the same: You may earn it, receive it, go home with it, but *you cannot play with it or eat it now. That is the rule.* It will solve other problems in your future days.

When you change the rules, it is frustrating to children.

4. The Incentive Must Excite The Children

Unfortunately, you cannot find anything you can afford as give-a-ways at a Christian book store. They are definitely a "for-profit" store. It all costs too much. So, you go to Kipp or Oriental Trading or U.S. Toy, for your incentives. Of course, small candy bags are inexpensive from Sam's Warehouse. With *"doo-dads, gadgets, and gizmos,"* you can often get ten thousand small items for ten bucks. It is stuff that no one on earth wants but a kid!

School supply stores have beautiful full-color card certificates for "pennies" a piece to offer your students. Colorful ribbons are for special recognition. You will find a multitude of recognition items there.

Your best of all prizes are reserved for special occasions, or the "best of the best." The reputation of your ***"Big Red Box"*** should be the talk of the kids as they walk in your door. What is in the ***"Big Red Box"*** this week? Nobody knows, but everybody wants whatever is in the box. Shake it, give hints, smell of it occasionally, go by it a couple of times just to see if it is still there. It drives them "nuts," but it also reminds them of your class rules to get it!

Your display of items should be exceptional. Do not display your prizes out of a beat-up card board box or a plastic bag from a local store. Put a table cloth on your table, a bright one. In other words, dress it up. This is one of the greatest incentives you have, and it can work for you the whole hour of class!

A larger item as a "grand prize" can work for you for 8-10 weeks. Maybe it is a $10 item you buy as a long range goal for someone to earn, based upon their own behavior over all the weeks. So, it will motivate all those weeks, and every week it will add to the beauty of your award table. Think - think - think!

5. The Involvement Games Must Be Fun

In a large group in a Children's Church setting (3-400 kids) I will have at least ten Bible games set up ready to go all over the auditorium. The games tie into the lesson and involve often 100 of the kids at the same time every time we have our break for a Bible game. One worker controls each game.

While the games continue, all the others are trying to earn the right to be chosen next (obeying the rules). *Master Ministries* has many excellent games, game books, overhead projector games, table-top card games, and power point games. Games can be chosen or ready for the regular church kids (fairly knowledgeable of Bible info) and some are simpler for the child who knows little to nothing about the Bible. You need both.

Bible games can be fun, while still teaching God's truth. They can teach the key verse you will center on in your lesson. A game covering the lesson you will teach today can motivate kids to listen well in order to win after the lesson, because they know it is coming! We call these *Bible Review Games.*

6. The "Hawkeyes" Must Be Fair

"Hawkeyes" look for good behavior, not bad. That is usually the very opposite of what we do. We look for bad behavior and assume that the good ones will be good. *Wrong!*

I met one teacher who would bring a bag of good cookies each week. However, the cookies were for those who misbehaved, offered as a treat to those who were misbehaving to stop their misbehavior. That worked for a few moments; until that child figured out that if I do it again I will get

> *The same children cannot win every time.*

another one. The children figured that one out, but the teacher never did see it. *Wrong!*

You must be fair, in this way: ***The same child or children cannot win every time,*** even if they are the best every time. If you award the same child or the same two or three every week, then the others know that. Some kids struggle to obey, because it is not how their home trained them. Some kids are lured by others who misbehave, some are hungry, some have home problems on their mind, and you would behave like they do if you were raised in their home. However, ***all kids have to know that they have a "chance" to win*** just like everyone else. If not, you have lost your best incentive.

If in a larger Children's Church setting, you must teach your workers this, and remind them often: you will always have one or two of the "perfect little angels," but you cannot afford for them to win every week. They win everywhere else they go, and everyone knows it. If a normally misbehaving child is better this week than he was last week, you had better pick him. No, he is still not perfect, but he is better than he was, and when he knows that he still has a "chance," he will improve again next week!

7. Misbehavior Cannot Continue

You cannot sacrifice the teaching of God's Word to your students because one child will not keep his mouth shut. You know you must do something about it. If not, then why cannot the others do the same? He/she may be keeping another child from being saved today or hearing a truth that they desperately need to hear. Something must be done, so what is it that you will do?

In a Children's Church setting, based on size, you may have two or more Hawkeyes who watch for misbehavior. In the smaller setting of a classroom you become both. So, some procedure must be the consistent rule here too. It should be pre-planned what the next step is, if the child will not stop. All teachers should have the same plan. It may be pre-arranged with the department head as to when the child is to be dismissed from a classroom. Bring it up, talk about it, and decide your plan. You must know, and the student should also know.

Any time you have six to eight different teachers in the same larger room, you have eight different personalities. We would all "handle" the same problem child a little differently. Some are like mush, some too hard, but there needs to be clear instructions as to what is our "middle ground," and let us all discipline the same way with the same consequences for wrong actions.

You do not have to "bark" at children.

A Few Closing Remarks:

Personally, I believe if the ***atmosphere*** is an exciting place for kids to come and the ***attitude*** of the teacher and workers is most pleasant, the behavior of the children will normally be the same. ***The positive over runs the negative.*** You do not have to "bark" at kids just to create a classroom that is a wonderful and colorful haven for children. ***Rules, yes, but presented in a positive way.*** If your incentive is good enough to convince the children they can play the games, gain points for their team, and win a prize before they go home, they will respond. I have enjoyed the benefits for many years! ***Remember:*** (1) <u>**You**</u> are one of the best incentives for good behavior. Your *attitude and your mannerisms* will create that good atmosphere for learning. (2) Everything you use, such as the attractiveness of your prize table, the prizes, the involvement games, etc., all are incentives. (3) Your content or lesson, your preparation and your presentation is a large incentive for students to listen and behave.

A Review of Key Thoughts:

1. One of the quotes in this chapter reminds us that "***Children*** are most like us in *feeling*, least like us in _____."

2. What technique has been called "The only painless form of learning"?

_____

3. Quiz yourself on two ways of "Getting ***adults*** to wake up more often:

(1) _____ (2) _____

_____

4. List three improvements to your own classroom:

(1) _____ (2) _____

(3) _____

5. In the section "The Discipline Of Children":

(1) Good Behavior Wins!

(2) The Rules Have To Be S_____

(3) The Rules Have To Be C_____

(4) The Incentives Must Excite The Kids

(5) The Involvement Games Must Be _____

(6) The "Hawkeyes" Must Be F_____

(7) Misbehavior C_____ Continue

Chapter NINE

Evaluating Or Verifying My Ministry Of Teaching!

For teachers, the thought of evaluating or verifying our ministry of teaching "should be" a welcome thought. However, it brings to mind those tests we took in school so often. We would rather assume our teaching is resulting in learning rather than knowing for sure. We can very easily assume for the next ten years, instead of knowing for sure. Facing reality is tough.

However, if we never know for sure, who does? But wait a minute, this involves the teaching of God's Word. The student's future is at stake. The clear communication of God's Word is at stake. The spiritual growth of your students is in question.

Sometimes the very thing that will help us greatly is somehow the thing we fear the most. Taking a good hard honest look at myself is harder than doing the same to someone else. But must do we must!

Let us look at the great value of evaluating or verifying our ministry. We should occasionally look at the scoreboard. Are we seeing our goals reached? If not, why not? If not, what changes are needed? We are looking for ways to improve our class. Just maintaining is not enough. There is no forward momentum in maintaining. So, let us force ourselves to look at ourselves (our preparation, our presentation), and be willing to improve. Evaluation does that!

We will also look at (1) The Teacher (2) The Classroom (3) The Student.

Evaluating Or Verifying My Ministry Of Teaching

1. Checking Your Results Leads To Greater Results

2. Evaluation Brings Great Value Now And For Our Future

3. Evaluation Reminds Me That It Is The Personal Touch I Need

4. Are We Seeing The Results We Seek?

5. Evaluation: What Is It?

6. Evaluation Initiates Greater Achievement

7. The Great Value Of Learning To Evaluate

8. Think Of It This Way. . .

(1) The Teacher   (2) The Classroom   (3) The Student

9. Fulfillment Comes To The Well-Prepared Teacher!

IX. Evaluating Or Verifying My Ministry Of Teaching

The goal here is not to make an inexhaustible list of 500 or more questions to use to see all the things you do not do well. We do want some standards that will help us to constantly improve our communicating skills. We need to occasionally measure our results, our effectiveness, and to verify if learning is taking place.

1. Checking your results leads to greater results. That is what every teacher needs, so look forward to improving your ability for the dear Lord!

Let this section be a great encouragement to you, not a threat. When you are through improving, your goals and dreams have come to a halt.

Allow me to first show some of the value of evaluating any work we are in, then we should see great need to face the facts. Then, we will set some standards by which we can make a judgment call on: (1) The teacher (2) The classroom (3) The student and learning.

Salvadore Diez-Verson, Jr. gave us a great thought, *"You don't become a better leader by changing other people; you become a better leader by improving yourself."*

2. Evaluation Brings Great Value Now And For Our Future

Here is where the teacher's honest desires to improve their teaching in order to enhance learning will need to stand up to the testing. We all would rather "assume" that we are much better than two years ago. That may be absolutely true. But, if teaching is concluded and learning has not taken place, so what?

This is God's work. It is His Word that we seek to help implant into real lives. It is not about us, it is about him/her (the student). It is about God's Word and all of us living in obedience there too. We have said before that we cannot make the student learn, but in our class they could learn, if they would learn.

So, our personal life-long goal of self-improvement as the teacher is the right goal to have. It was **Winston Churchill** who said, "No matter how beautiful the strategy, you should occasionally look at the results."

3. Evaluation Reminds Me That It Is The Personal Touch I Need

Sometimes, this becomes hard to face. But facing it will drive us to sharpen our abilities. It may even bring us to realize that the one hour or less per week we teach is just not enough. Where is the personal touch? Where is the time I seek to get into the student's life? When is it that I show I care about him as an everyday person with all the failures and all the temptations he faces? He lives in the real world, just like everyone else. He only lives in your classroom for one hour a week, at best.

Your student hears the jokes told at school or the office, he watches a myriad of TV shows. The teen is bombarded by whatever is pushing his peer group this year. The adult has many options at work to test the real Christian life and its values.

The area we deal with here involves our students. With every age group of students, learning more about the Bible is a goal, but not the larger goal of having their life changed forever!

4. Are We Seeing The Results We Seek?

We cannot fear looking at our report card. Those of you who were "straight A's" never felt like some of us did when it was time to take that report card home. It was a different feeling, close to agony. For some of us whose Dad had a *"woodshed,"* the agony went all the way to the seat of our pants. Those of us who were always "borderline cases" did not want to look, much more to have Mom and Dad look. But, look we must.

Face reality, God is not angry at us, but he always requires looking at the results. The big test for the child of God is still to come; it is called the **Judgment Seat of Christ.** Again, each of us will have to take a look at the stewardship we gave to the ministry of teaching that He gave to us.

But out of the gracious heart of God He tells us in His Word some 50,60,70 years in advance: Romans 14:10-12; Hebrews 9:27 "And it is appointed unto men once to die, but after this the judgment." From a young child, and now so many years later, the Lord has reminded me. When I return to the "hills" I still see the signs tacked on the roadside trees, "Prepare To Meet Thy God." I guess I was no more than five or six years old when I first asked Dad what the sign meant. I have been warned multiple times and for many years.

5. Evaluation: What It Is!

Evaluation is an attitude of improving my position from adequate to excellent! The better attitude is this: "I can't wait to find a better more productive way than how I do it now!" That kind of attitude pushes me to schedule evaluation times on my calendar. I really cannot wait for the next one. What if I could do it better, using another method next week? Surely I would want to know what is better. That is what awaits me at the end of my evaluation!

Maintaining where we are is not the goal of our classroom forever. There is no "push" in just maintaining. There is no forward momentum, no greater heights to achieve. Evaluation forces me to face reality. I need that to push me.

6. Evaluation Initiates Greater Achievement

Caring enough to evaluate your own ministry to the Lord and to also verify the learning of your students puts you in the highest level of teachers, because most never do. Thinking your ministry through is always up to you.

I have for years been a fan of *Walt Disney*, the original man and his most creative mind. He learned early on to think well. In his book ***Creating Magic*** by Lee Cockerell, he says of his boss, "Walt Disney didn't wait for employees or customers to complain about hassles *(hassles referred to deficient service to guests)* before he re-evaluated his processes. As a great leader always should, he looked for ways to improve how things are done because 'We've always done it that way' could mean that you've been doing it wrong all along." *(Parenthesis added)*.

That is how we should feel about our personal teaching and our classroom. ***Stop along the way for no other purpose than to improve yourself for your students!***

Coming from a very small town in the "hills," I never thought about evaluation or other big words. After college, I still had not learned well to evaluate. But, once I learned from others how to have a *"think time,"* evaluation has been a great partner in every undertaking since that day!

7. The Great Value Of Learning To Evaluate

Peter Daniels, an internationally acclaimed businessman, a billionaire, when asked what made the difference for him, said, *"I scheduled time to think. In fact I reserve one day a week on my calendar just to think. All of my greatest ideas, opportunities and money-making ventures started with the days I took off to think!"*

Did you hear that? Fifty-two whole days a year just to think! Now, turn your eyes toward the church of the living God, and take another look at your role for the Lord. Does not your time, given by God, deserve your scheduling time to "think it through" for the work of the Lord?

Evaluation or verifying learning helps you to face reality. If you are unable to face the truth, problems seem to last forever. Understanding your bottom line is the difference between where you are now and where you could be in six months or a year from now! Find out for yourself what it is that will make a great difference for you: (1) What if you spent two additional hours per week in preparation? (2) What if you read two books this year on teaching your age group? (3) What if you bought a new marker board for your class? (4) What if you increased your personal teaching library (add two books, add the Teacher's Quick Reference guide, or add two object lesson books, etc.)?

Evaluation is a sign of leadership, yours! It is a leader who anticipates improving. You must anticipate growing your own class. Do not settle back to wait for each new visitor to come in on a bus. *Without an anticipation of Sunday school growth, then the whole church will need no more room, no chairs, no more teachers, no follow-up tools, and few to none salvations will be seen.*

Here is a good thought from *Dr. Howard Hendricks,* *"Experience doesn't make you better. Only evaluated experience makes you better."*

Evaluation means that you have a passion to do a greater work than has been done to date. It is that fire that burns within. It is that drive that will not allow you to slip into a maintenance mindset.

Dr. Clarence Sexton, founder of Crown College said, *"Your failure to lead is greater than the people's failure to follow."*

8. Think Of It This Way. . .

Obviously that thought covers about all the bases in the leadership of the church. If I could tweak it toward the role of teaching itself, I might say it this way, *"Your failure to evaluate your own teaching is greater than the student's disinterest."* Or I might say it another way: *"The blaming of students for my woes in the classroom has more to do with me than them."*

Am I leading but no one is following? Am I teaching but there is no visible response to learning? Evaluation pushes me to take a good long honest look, then change, if need be. You do not dread the next time to stop and think it over. Without evaluation for your classroom and your students you may simply repeat your ineffective methods over and over.

How can I lead my class if I refuse to think things through about my own effectiveness? If I could lead or teach my class better than now, why would I not want to get to that point? Evaluation is intentional self-motivation. It is planning spots of time to take stock of what is working and what is not working. If it is not working, then why am I still doing it? I need to know that.

When I evaluate my students, it helps me to value my students more. When I evaluate or verify my student's learning, it makes me stop and think. Thinking is where the next answer comes from. That is who you are and what you do – and it is a wonderful way to serve the Lord!

Thanks for staying with me in this trip through what I feel is an urgency for us all to understand the value of this review we call evaluation or to verify learning. Now, let us look at a few ways to verify what is happening in this ministry that we give a big portion of our life to.

Look at the following as a starting place. You can add to the list as you see the value of evaluation, and as you continue the drive to get better for your Lord!

(1) The Teacher

Spiritual goals should be high on my list as a teacher. What are your goals for your students? None? There must be! Use the Discipleship Roll book to keep up with each student, consistently reminding yourself of the needs as you prepare for the next week's lesson.

At what level of commitment are you to teaching? Take a personal (your eyes only) quiz?

This is my present level of commitment (Check One)

_____ I will teach on Sunday, but other than that don't bother me.

_____ I will teach and maybe I will visit once a month or so, but that's it.

_____ I will do the above, plus I will read one book this year to improve myself. Don't ask for more.

_____ Since this ministry is the biggest thing I do for God and to honor God, I will whole-heartedly. . .

_____

_____

_____

This is my commitment to God and to my church.

Sign _____

How is your *emptiness*, your *filling of God's Spirit*, your *preparedness* each week, your *prayer life* during the week by name and by need? How is your *faith*? Are you seeing *increase by faith*? If not, why not?

In other words, think through from your week of preparation to the end of your class. Learn to ask yourself some *hard questions* and make yourself come up with an answer. After all, evaluation is about you and your students, not the class next door to yours. Learn to "push yourself," even if there is no accountability to another in your church structure; remember that ultimately you face God!

(2) The Classroom

Does your classroom teach? The teaching tools of a Bible teacher should at least rival that of a school teacher. What grabs the attention during those non-teaching moments? What is it that if seen repetitively for the next six weeks would remain fixed in the minds of your students? If not anything, why not? If not, when? If your church supplies no visual aid room or supplies, a School supply store will be like a "gold mine" for you!

Is your classroom colorful? Not just for kids, but how about the teen or adult room?

Is your room dull? Paint it! No classroom should look like a flea market.

Is your room organized? Are all your notes ready? Late arriving teachers mess up a whole lot of things. When the students beat you to class, it is a sad day.

Is your classroom out of date? Are Christmas decorations still up in March? Shame. Shame.

Is your classroom clean? There is no excuse for a dirty classroom, none.

Do you ever sit in their seat, just to take a look around the room to see what they see?

(3) The Student

What do you consistently see in the *mannerisms* of your students (eye contact or the lack of gestures, body language, responses to questions)? What does that teach you about the individual (yes, even adults)? Remember that you have mannerisms, but so do they! Do you know much about the student outside of class?

What is missing in a child or teen's life? What Biblical characteristics are missing or hard to see in certain students? Is the student serving the Lord? Do you see a decreasing of sin in their life? If not, why? How often do you *encourage* your students, as in individual contact, not just a group word?

How about your personal role-model before your students? Do they see the truth in your life?

Start with some of these questions, then add or subtract until every time you stop to verify learning it becomes great gain for you!

With teens or adults an annual quick survey may be of help in your evaluation. Think of the type of questions you would like to ask a teen or adult, but you know they probably would not want to give you an answer face to face. Even though you can have them leave their name off, make sure they understand that this will greatly help you to improve yourself and your class time. No false questions or suggestions or answers will be accepted. Express your earnest desire.

Look back down in time to six-months ago. Now do I see change?

Never forget that the *personal visit* and conversation shows to the student that you are serious about them, the classroom, and their teaching to go out of your way to ask for their comments!

9. Fulfillment Comes To The Well-Prepared Teacher!

Once you have had that good taste of fulfillment, you want it again. Fulfillment fills! That is well worth the conscious effort to *push yourself*!

Many who have honed their skills for forty-years in a career or trade, find it extremely hard to retire to a life of leisure. It may be a novelty for six months or so, but often the "itch" comes back. Something is missing in life, and I believe that often that feeling of fulfillment is not there any more. The "honey-do" lists have all been done and there is little on the list for the next day.

We are seeing more missionaries go to the fields of the world at later ages than ever before. They have had their careers (fulfilling) but now at 55, 60, 65 years of age they just do not want to stop. Their skills are at their highest level. Experience has weeded out most of the youthful mistakes. Why not spend the rest of your life active, alive, energetic, and fulfilled? It is a big question, and once you answer it, there is *Your Push!*

What is fulfillment for you? Whatever it is for you, it will not arrive without your striving toward that goal. It will probably require some mastery on your part. But, even finding mastery brings fulfillment!

For example, if you are a teacher, fulfillment does not come by preparing "just enough" to get by next week. Eventually, guilt will come instead of that wonderful feeling of fulfillment.

Your preparation, studying, planning, preparing, will make your presentation fulfilling. The lack or the slack in preparation brings less than fulfillment. Oh, others may compliment you on a good lesson or good class, but you know deep down inside it was no where near your best. Your best takes effort and fulfillment does not come from less than your best. The joy of striving and mastering brings the greatest feeling of all.

I have met so many over the years who give the same account, "I went to College for a year or two or even three, but never finished." Everyone without exception follow quickly by saying, "but I wish to this day that I had finished my goal." And for some that was forty years ago, and they are still wishing things had turned out differently. It is still "gnawing" at them.

In my teacher training sessions I have yet to put it all on DVDs. I have been asked to often, and perhaps I will. But for me, it has all been wrapped up in that feeling of fulfillment. I have always traveled to each training site for a reason. I want to bring all the books, teaching aids, posters, and visuals with me so teachers can see. I lug boxes of books they can buy. The power point presentation is a necessity. I carry my own large screen, computer, and projector just to make sure it is right. It takes me four hours to set up the auditorium. But, most of all I prefer a live session so I can put some feeling, emotion, expression, and loads of passion in what I have to say. I want them to feel, hear, and see just how significant the principles of teaching really are.

One of my visuals is a very bright thermometer called "The Teacher Significance O'Meter." Every few pages the thermometer gives a loud "Whooosh" and goes up another notch. It reinforces their significance in the classroom.

For me, the whole plan is what brings fulfillment. I am sure the day is coming when all of that is too much for me to handle, and I dread it. That is when I am at my best. That is fulfillment. That is what has driven me to keep on *Pushing Myself!* Every week, just before the session begins, I am in a back room somewhere doing my "self-talk." I am trying to *Push Myself!* It is a reminder again of the purpose of teacher training; it is why I am here. They need what they are about to get. It will help them greatly. I cannot wait! By the time the introduction is finished by a pastor, I am about to explode. If he goes a bit too long I walk closer as if to say "Let's move!"

For you, whatever the career, you know there is a best level of performance, and there is a less than your best. What is it going to be? *Push Yourself!*

A Review Of Key Thoughts:

1. Quote: "You don't become a better leader by changing other people; you become a better leader by improving _____."

2. Winston Churchill said, "No matter how beautiful the strategy, you should occasionally look _____ _____ _____."

3. The Bible reminds us that of the biggest evaluation of our entire life – it is called the _____ _____ of _____.

4. There is no "_____" in just maintaining.

5. "Your failure to evaluate your own teaching is greater than the student's _____."

6. Did you "up" your commitment level after the survey? Yes _____ No _____

Chapter TEN

Heaven! For Sure And Forever!

Although written in the context of sharing Christ with children, the content here would benefit you if your age group is in *teens or adults*. I encourage you to center your attention on the few pages. One of the great purposes of our teaching for all ages is life-change. The biggest of all life-changes brings salvation to all who believe!

In this age, never assume that even teens or adults have a clear understanding of words and terms about salvation. These seven short chapters will give you some good ideas!

Heaven! For Sure And Forever!

1. All Children Have A Right To Go To Heaven!

2. Salvation- The Issue Is Belief Or Unbelief.

3. Fields Are Extremely White- "Unto Harvest"!

4. Make Much Of Jesus!

5. Always Use Question/Answer

6. In The Middle Of Going- Walk Carefully

7. What Confuses Children?

The following last chapter has been extracted from a previous book entitled *Sharing Christ With Children! by Abb Thomas.*

1. All Children Have A Right To Go To Heaven!

Jesus straightened out our thinking about allowing children to come to Him. While His disciples seemed irritated with little children, Jesus cleared up their thinking as well:

> *"But Jesus said, Suffer (allow) little children, and forbid them not,*
> *to come unto me: for of such is the kingdom of heaven."*
> *Matthew 19:14 (parenthesis added)*

In this day and time, when sin is seeking its beach head in very young lives, we (the church) must be more aggressive than ever before. Someone must get up out of the pew and take the message of Christ to children and to all ages.

Children have many strikes against them:
1. The world and its system is more aggressive than ever before in going after our children (drugs, sex, sitcoms, MTV, etc.)
2. Many are raised in ungodly and unconcerned homes.
3. Millions are raised in "religion" but not in Christ.

4. The philosophies of elementary schools impact the child 5 days each week.

5. Even the "Christian" home, where the child is raised seeing no reality of what a true believer is or does. A "form of godliness" totally confuses the child. There are multiple thousands of "twenties" or young marrieds who are still confused from a home with a "form of godliness."

If we allow children, in this day, to go through their childhood years without the Savior, we have real problems on our hands. Children see and hear the world's philosophy of life almost daily – the home, school, and television literally "show and tell" its way of life over and over. It takes a great toll on these young lives, well before the teen years. The battle for the heart of a child is *before* the age of fourteen.

Unless we *out-race* the world for the mind and heart of the child, it just may be too difficult to overcome. Why risk it? Why not counteract the bad with the good. Yes, God will save the worst of them all- at 15, 25, 45, or 105- if they will come to Him.

After fourteen years of age, statistically only a few ever come to Christ. We cannot deny the influence of this world.

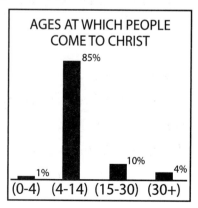

AGES AT WHICH PEOPLE COME TO CHRIST

85%

10%

4%

1%

(0-4) (4-14) (15-30) (30+)

Jesus told His disciples plainly, and for all of us of all ages to come, "Suffer little children, and forbid them not. . ." Allow them to come, now – today, AS a little child.

"And that from a child thou hast known the holy scriptures, which are able to make thee wise unto salvation though faith which is in Christ Jesus." II Timothy 3:15

Right now, as a child, let them hear the Holy Scriptures. Allow them to be included in the invitation. Do no forbid them to come. Shame on us, if we make the decisions of children of less significance than older people.

The Savior came for the purpose of giving all men the opportunity to be saved from their sins. Since Christ did all the necessary work, the least we can do is to tell children. Someone, somehow, on some day told you the wonderful story of Jesus! Does not every person on earth deserve to hear?

"For whosoever shall call upon the name of the Lord shall be saved. How then shall they call on him in whom they have not believed? and how shall they believe in him of whom they have not heard? and how shall they hear without a preacher?"
Romans 10:13-14

God's wonderful promise of *salvation still must be heard,* and we are still the ones whom God has chosen to proclaim it. For millions of children, the parents will not tell; the neighbors will not tell; the close-by churches will not tell; and unless you go, the child will never hear.

Without your church being aggressive in taking out the message of Jesus, the very folks around you will never hear until it may be so late they refuse to hear. The bad has overwhelmed the good in their young minds.

In a day where literally thousands of churches have sold their buses, how will the children hear? In all honesty, they will not. Thy cannot drive as yet, their parents will not bring them, church members will not even try, we have stopped bussing them in – *how do we expect them to hear?* The problem is, we do not expect them to hear, and it does not bother us any more anyway. That is a major problem- a spiritual problem. *The problem is us,* and seemingly, we have no plans for fixing the problem.

In Fairbanks, Alaska, where I have been three times, one church uses sixteen buses. Why? Because buses still bring in those who could not come without the church helping. I asked, "In all the cold of winter, when do you consider not running the buses?" Their answer, "When it gets to -40°F we will begin discussing it." That is a church with a heart for God, and for children.

> ## "Go for souls, and go for the worst."
> ## William Booth

Perhaps we should read again the life and times of William Booth, founder of the Salvation Army. When the "main stream" churches of his day rejected those who needed it most, his constant cry was **"Go for souls, and go for the worst."** His own church forced him to bring the "down-and-outers" to enter the back door and sit where they could not be seen. Are we really any better then they?

I once heard a Pastor say, "The only reason we run buses, is because my people will not bring anybody. My people come to church with an empty back seat." I would dare say that is the problem in 99% of our churches today, even our evangelistic churches. We all know we "ought to," but we just fail to do what we ought to be doing.

When kids do not have an opportunity to hear a clear presentation of the Gospel, *it is our fault, not theirs.* The last command that Jesus gave to His church was to **Go and make disciples.**

Jesus gave His command then turned it over to his followers to "work out the details." Is your church working out the details? If not, why not? If not, when? We have the Gospel message, right inside our Bible. But children do not know that, unless someone tells them. So, I must take that message "out there," if they will not come to our church. Or, somehow I must attract them to church where they can hear the wonderful news of Christ!

Therefore, I ask myself, what is on our church calendar in the next three months that will get us "up and out of the pew" and out to where "little" sinners live? Or, what is on our calendar to attract them to us? We should be doing both. Children have a right to know!

The Gospel Is A Cost Of Discipleship
"For whosoever will save his life shall lose it;
but whosoever shall lose his life for my sake
and the gospel's, the same shall save it."
Mark 8:35

The Gospel Demands Going
"And how shall they preach, except they be sent?
As it is written, How beautiful are the feet of them

that preach the gospel of peace, and bring glad
tidings of good things." Romans 10:15

The Gospel Demands A Confrontation
"In whom the god of this world hath blinded the minds of them
which believe not, lest the light of the glorious gospel of Christ,
who is the image of God, should shine unto them."
II Corinthians 4:4

The Gospel Demands A Presentation
"And he said unto them, Go ye into all the world, and
preach the gospel to every creature."
Mark 16:15

So, fellow Christian worker, those same demands are upon us. Will we, or will we not take the glorious Gospel message to the folks in our own outreach area? Someday, at a place called the Judgment Seat of Christ, He will bring all this up again. Our stewardship of His Word to children will come into question. The Lord will bring this matter up again.

Therefore, I suggest that we all take another hard look at our aggressiveness, or the lack of it. Are children without Christ more accessible to us 10,000 miles across the sea, or three miles down the road? We have already raised our support, we know the language, transportation and communication is

Are children without Christ more accessible to us 10,000 miles away, or three miles down the road?

good, we are already working
out of a local church, so what is our problem?

For you and me, *disobedience is our problem.*

How are we doing? Look at your church calendar. Does it reveal plans to get the Gospel out? If not, why not? If not now, when?

As leaders, we must learn to ask ourselves those hard questions, and make ourselves come up with an answer. Steal away to a lone bedroom, look in a mirror at yourself and respond to these questions: If not, why not? If not, when? Is what we are doing still working?

Children have a right to go to Heaven! But they will never hear apart from our aggressive outreach. They will never understand without a clear presentation of the Gospel. Both are our part of the Gospel of Christ. *The Lord chose us* to get the job done!

Our Christian world is appalled at the thought of abortion. How could anyone conclude that it is all right to take away a baby's opportunity for life?

Yet, how can we feel no regret for taking away a child's right to spiritual life? Yes, it is a choice, his choice. But, does he have the right to at least hear the option that is available to him of eternal life?

Is that not exactly what our assignment is in our "Jerusalem"? Most of them do not know there is a choice between life and death. Millions of parents will never tell them. Hundreds of other churches will never tell them. They will never hear it at school. So, what are their chances where you live? Children have a right to go to Heaven!

2. Salvation – The Issue Is Belief/ Sin – The Issue Is Unbelief

If the sin problem is *unbelief*, then the salvation solution is *belief*.

In reality, sin carries the sentence of death and Hell forever. The only possible way out of the problem is to believe in the death, burial, and resurrection of God's Son. He is our only substitute who can pay the high cost of sin through His own shed blood, " The blood of Jesus Christ his Son cleanseth us from all sin." *I John 1:7b*

We try to say it so clearly: It is by grace, through faith, that salvation takes place. Through His grace, salvation is offered to all who believe.

"For the wages of sin is death;	**B** **U** **T**	**the gift of God is eternal life through Jesus Christ our Lord." Romans 6:23**

1. The sin is unbelief

I was born a sinner, which is why I sin. Then I grow to an age when I continuously understand that it is **my** sin and that it is **against God.**

I believe we need to make much out of sin. It begins by understanding that the sin of unbelief is where we all start. It is the *prayer of the sinner.* For the child, when they come to that age of understanding, it is the *prayer of belief* that saves.

**"That whosoever believeth in him, should not perish,
but have everlasting life."**

Sometimes our emphasis is on the wrong sin(s).

Teaching in a Christian College, I asked ten students to prepare an eight minute witnessing presentation. Without exception, all ten took the same approach. As if witnessing to a child (they demonstrated on a fellow student), each "soulwinner" started off explaining sin. Have you ever sinned? "Uhh, I guess so," said the partner. Well, have you ever told a lie? "Well, sure." Have you ever said bad words? "Sure, everybody does." Well then, you are on your way to Hell. If belief is the difference between Heaven and Hell, why do we describe sin to children as doing bad things, such as lying, stealing, disobedience to parents, etc? Are these sins? Sure they are. But, does doing bad things take one to Hell? No. Does lying take one to Hell? No. Does cursing or a multitude of other sins damn us to be apart from God forever? In reality, it is the *sin of unbelief* that is the real problem.

2. Get to the main issue and stay there.

I believe we would be better off dealing with the issue of **unbelief.**

"He that *believeth* **on him (Jesus) is not condemned:
but he that** *believeth* **not is condemned already,
because he hath** *not* **believed in the name of the only
begotten Son of God." John 3:18 (parenthesis added)**

HE THAT BELIEVETH – That Is The Issue.

Now, to *"personalize"* that truth to the child, bring it down to where God is talking to him. Read it like this, adding his name in each blank:

> ***If (Joey)*** *believeth* **on him (Jesus)** ***(Joey)***
> ***is not condemned: but if*** ***(Joey)*** *believeth not*
> ***(Joey)*** *is condemned already, because* ***(Joey)***
> **hath** *not believed* **in the name of the only begotten**
> **Son of God."**

3. Use a series of verses to illustrate sin.

Clearly show that sin is a **choice.**

John 3:18 "He that believeth on Him is not condemned: but he that believeth not (a choice is made) is condemned already, because he hath not believed (a choice) in the name of the only begotten Son of God."

John 3:15 (a choice is made).

John 1:12 (a choice to receive Christ).

Romans 10:13 (a choice is made).

To Believe Is A Choice. . . Not To Believe Is A Choice. . .A Big Choice!

"That whosoever BELIEVETH in Him should not perish. . ."

John 3:15 – **Not to believe is to perish**

"For God so loved the world, that he gave his only begotten Son, that whosoever BELIEVETH in him should not perish. . ." John 3:16 – **Not to believe is to perish**

"He that BELIEVETH on the Son hath everlasting life. . ." John 3:36 "and he that BELIEVETH NOT the Son shall not see life. . ." – **Not to believe is to not see life.**

John chapter 3 is another great series of verses that give emphasis to believing. It is always the choice of believing or not believing.

We covered some of these verses before, but let us remind ourselves again how clearly God's Word makes it.

"That whosoever *believeth in him* should not perish, but have eternal life." John 3:15	"For God so loved the world, that he gave his only begotten Son, that whosoever *believeth in him* should not perish, but have everlasting life." John 3:16
"He that *believeth on him* is not condemned: but he that *believeth not*. . ." 3:18	"He that *believeth on the Son* hath everlasting life: and he that *believeth not* the Son shall not see life. . ." 3:36
He that *believeth, believeth, believeth, believeth*. . . Sounds like the Lord is trying to focus us!	

4. The three crosses picture both the problem and the solution.

In the Three Crosses booklet (available from MasterClubs.org), we use the visible picture of the crosses to help show the two extremes. One man died in his sin. The only Savior he would ever have was only a few feet away, yet he made the choice to curse God's Son, and he died like that. So, what happens when a person dies without the Savior? Now, we proceed to explain what the debt of sin brings to the sinner. Wages bring what we have earned. Anyone can understand what it means to work to

earn wages. The wages for one's sin is death. Stop right there! What does death mean? All can understand physical death, but is spiritual death the same thing? No, the spirit of man does not die, so what is the difference?

We need to explain that death brings a separation. What happens to a person who has not believed on the Lord Jesus Christ? The illustration here helps to explain the word death in Romans 6:23. The question is, why would I just quote the verse and "assume" that an unsaved child (or adult) would naturally understand the real truth of this verse?

"For God so loved the world, that he gave his only begotten Son, that whosoever believeth in him should not <u>PERISH</u>, but have everlasting life." John 3:16	**To PERISH means...** **To die *without* God** **To go to a place *without* God** **To be forever *without* God**

It is better to assume nothing, and plan on thoroughly explaining such words in the verses you use. As illustrated here, emphasize the WITHOUT of these thoughts. The idea of separation from God forever is the really bad news.

5. The second area we move into in the Three Crosses booklet is the Savior who died for the two men in sin.

Children need to understand who died for the man in sin. They need to thoroughly understand that: (1) Christ is the only Savior.(2) Christ is willing and able to forgive sin. (3) Christ saves us from sin when we believe in Him! Make much of Christ. Without His cross-work, we have no message to give. Without their belief in Him little ones have no Savior, no redeemer, and no payment for sin.

6. Notes on the death of God's Son.

The death of Jesus Christ included both His death and His blood. *Without death,* there would be no victory over death, hell, and the grave. His power over death and the grave was proven by His resurrection. *Without blood,* there would be no cleansing flow that washes white as snow.

We do not necessarily have to go into a long explanation of the cruelty Jesus was exposed to, the crown of thorns, whipping, slapping, pulling out of the beard, etc., to explain salvation. They will hear all of that later in messages and lessons. They need to know that the death, burial, resurrection of Jesus Christ makes Him the Savior, and the only Savior for the whole world. They need Jesus!

Christ, The One Who Saves From Sin
Beautiful Verses To Reveal Christ The Savior

Here is a partial list of Christ as Savior verses. Pick out the one or two that seem best for you and insert into your own plan of salvation to a child.

No Other Name- Acts 4:12 "Neither is there salvation in any other: for there is <u>none other name</u> under heaven given among men, whereby we must be saved."	**One God – One Way- I Tim. 2:5** "For there is <u>one God, and one mediator</u> between God and men, the man Christ Jesus."
Himself For Our Sins- Gal. 1:4 "Who gave <u>himself for our sins,</u> that he might deliver us from this present evil world, according to the will of God and our Father."	**He Bare Our Sins- I Peter 2:24** "Who his own self <u>bare our sins</u> in his own body on the tree. . ."
Christ Died For Sins- I Cor. 15:3 "For I delivered unto you first of all that which I also received, how that <u>Christ died for our sins</u> according to the scriptures."	**To Be Sin For Us- II Cor. 5:21** "For he hath made him <u>to be sin for us,</u> who knew no sin; that we might be made the righteousness of God in him."
Christ Died For Us- Romans 5:6 "For when we were yet without strength, in due time <u>Christ died for the ungodly.</u>"	**Saved Through Him- John 3:17** "For God sent not his Son into the world to condemn the world; but that the world <u>through him might be saved.</u>"
God Gives Eternal Life- I John. 5:11 "And this is the record, that God hath <u>given to us eternal life</u>, and this life is in his Son."	**Gift Of Eternal Life- John 10:28** "And <u>I give unto them eternal life</u>; and they shall never perish. . ."
Shall Never Die- John 11:26 "And whosoever liveth and <u>believeth in me</u> shall never die. Believeth thou this?"	**Way- Truth- Life- John 14:6** "Jesus saith unto him, I am the way, the truth, and the life: no man cometh unto the Father, but by me."

Son To Be The Savior-I John 4:14 "And we have seen and do testify that the Father <u>sent the Son to be the Savior</u> of the world."	**Christ's Blood- Ephesians 1:7** "In whom we have redemption <u>through his blood</u>, the forgiveness of sins. . ."
Receive Him- John 1:12 "But as many <u>as received him</u>, to them gave he power to become the. . ."	**Knowing For Sure That I Know Him- I John 5:11-13**

7. The third cross shows that belief saves.

There was a third cross on Calvary. Through this cross we see anther choice. This man, also about to die "in his sin," made a different choice. It would mean a different location, forever. It meant the opposite direction, opposite destiny, and the difference between joy and immense sorrow forever. His choice was to believe, the opposite of unbelief.

But, just to say *believe* to a child who has never believed on the Lord may not be enough help. The Hindus and Muslims believe. Believe what? Believe Who? The verse covered earlier (John 3:18) could help you to personalize the truth of believing in the Lord Jesus (If <u>(Joey)</u> believeth on him. . .)

Since using the Three Crosses idea, going from unbelief to belief, then we are saying: Explain that carefully, without adding confusing issues. It is unbelief that does the damage. It is belief that saves us from sin forever. Explain it slowly and carefully. Use questions to see if the child understands, then move on.

3. Fields Are Extremely White- "Unto Harvest"

Many Christian workers may tend to skip over this chapter, as though "I already know that." But, please read on as it may give you a greater burden to transfer the same feelings to your fellow workers.

Never become weary of reading **Matthew 9:35-38.** It is a passage to inspire us, to remind us, to help us see as Jesus did when He walked this earth. It is encouraging, not discouraging. Sometimes we "hang up" on the "laborers are few," and miss the encouragement that the harvest truly is "plenteous"!

"And Jesus went about all the cities and villages, teaching in their synagogues, and preaching the gospel of the kingdom and healing every sickness and every disease among the people.

But when he saw the multitudes, he was moved with compassion on them, because they fainted, and were scattered abroad, as sheep having no shepherd.

Then saith he unto his disciples, The harvest truly is plenteous, but the laborers are few;

Pray ye therefore the Lord of the harvest, that he will send forth

"when he saw . . . he was moved with compassion

Do I see? Am I moved?

laborers into his harvest." Matthew 9:35-38

We see here two great extremes:

| PLENTEOUS | FEW |

How plenteous is our field? Look up and down your street next Sunday, on your way to church. Would you say there are at least 80% of the families around you who never go to church? Not too many streets in America would be the exception. As of this writing the larger surveys remind us that 84% of adults did not go to church last Sunday. The fields are **PLENTEOUS!**

Christianity is growing on every continent on earth except in North America. The fields are **PLENTEOUS!**

Seventy percent of church growth is by transfer or biological growth. We are not growing from new converts. The fields are **PLENTEOUS!**

Every street, almost every house, the fields are **PLENTEOUS!**

Our *outreach* must change. Our *thinking* must change. Our *"prospecting"* must increase. What will it take and how will we accomplish reaching the plenteous in our area? We must study well and understand the demographics in our area. Think of this in light of seeing the graph that shows 85% of ages 4-14 are the ones who come to Christ. Yet, 80% of our evangelism dollar is spent on adult evangelism, with few visible results. That leaves only 20% of every dollar set for evangelism is put into the most fruitful

> *Child evangelism is where the fruit is!*

ministry of all, that of children and teens.

Child evangelism is where the fruit is! We should have the best tools available, the biggest campaigns, the most prospecting, and the greatest inspiring sermons to reach the most fruitful mission field!

Every pastor must answer to this overwhelming fact of the most fruitful potential of children. We cannot allow children to go through their childhood years without Christ. The dear Lord will bring into question *our stewardship* of getting the gospel to children. Allow them to come to Christ early. It is our *greatest* potential, our *highest* of prospects, our *most* plenteous field, and our *most* fruitful area. Therefore, the largest potential for ministry in our church!

We sometimes get our thinking reversed. We all stand around waiting for our attendance to get better, and it never does. We are too often starting backwards. The scenario is this- We all "hope" some visitors will come next week, but nobody knows who it will be. We have no new names, no new faces, or addresses. Sure enough, they did not come.

Dear Christian worker, we must believe that outreach is non-negotiable, and that the Great Commission is exactly God's will for my church, my class, and my own personal obedience to God's Word.

Do we have a strategy to see the Great Commission fulfilled or not? Do we just "assume" it is going to happen? You would not run a business by hoping or just assuming, would you?

The bottom line is this: Without teachers going after prospects, there will be no growth, no converts, and no one to hear the gospel.

4. Make Much Of Jesus!!

ONE GOD- ONE CREATOR- ONE SAVIOR- ONE HEAVEN

<u>**ALL INCLUSIVE!**</u>

**"For whosoever shall call upon the name
of the Lord shall be saved." Romans 10:13**

Jesus is the solution, the Good News, the problem solver, the Way, the Truth, the Life, the Almighty, the Redeemer, Advocate, Sustainer, Counselor, and so much more! And, He is this and more for **WHOSOEVER** will come!

He is the Savior of this child!
He is the Way to Heaven!
He is the solution for our sins!
It is His love, grace, and mercy toward us!
It is His blood that brings remission of our sin!
It is His death that paid our sin price!
It is His Divine Plan!

*Make much
of Jesus!*

The younger the child, the more important the "invitation" becomes. Younger ages have such a love for the teacher that their decision can easily be just an agreement with the teacher. As counselors to our children, we must go to extremes to insure that they understand it is a prayer to God, not just to please the teacher. Make much of Jesus! Children can understand that. The Bible is full of verses like those below. Perhaps you need to use some of these verses in place of some you use already.

"That whosoever believeth <u>in him</u> (Jesus) should not perish but have eternal life."
John 3:15
It's Jesus!

"For God so loved the world, that he gave his only begotten Son, that whosoever believeth <u>in him</u> should not perish, but have everlasting life."
John 3:16
It's Jesus!

"For God sent not his Son into the world to condemn the world; but that the world <u>through him</u> might be saved." John 3:17
It's Jesus!

"He that believeth <u>on him</u> (Jesus) is not condemned. . ." John 3:18a
It's Jesus!

"He that believeth <u>on the Son</u> hath everlasting life. . ."
John 3:36a
It's Jesus!

"For there is one God, and one mediator between God and men, the man <u>Christ Jesus</u>."
I Timothy 2:5
It's Jesus!

"For he (God) hath made <u>him</u> (Jesus) <u>to be sin</u> for us. . ."
II Corinthians 5:21a
It's Jesus!

"Who gave <u>himself</u> for our sins, that he might deliver us from this present evil world. . ."
Galatians 1:4a
It's Jesus!

"Jesus saith unto him, I am the <u>way</u>, the <u>truth</u>, and the <u>life</u>; no man cometh unto the Father but <u>by me</u>!"
John 14:6
It's Jesus!

"For Christ also hath once suffered for sins, the just for the unjust, that he might bring us to God."
I Peter 3:18a   **It's Jesus!**

Make much of Jesus!

The tree of everlasting life!

"have **eternal** life"

John 3:15

"have **everlasting** life"

John 3:16

"shall **never die**"   "hath **everlasting** life"   "this is **life eternal**"

John 11:26   *John 3:36*   *John 17:3*

"shall **live forever**"

John 6:58

Promise after promise after promise is given to those who believe!

"unto them **eternal** life"

John 10:28

"to us **eternal** life"

I John 5:11

"ye have **eternal** life"

I John 5:13

5. Always Use Question/Answer

Any teacher who involves the student in active listening would testify to the value of asking questions and waiting for answers.

A huge question for any counselor is this- ***Does he really understand?*** You will never know for sure if you do not ask the child. Ask the right kind of question, and the child will tell you whether or not he understands.

Avoid the head nod in agreement with you, for it tells you very little. Kids often agree with adults when actually they have no clear idea of the answer.

You need to understand if he understands,

then you can go on.

Ask a question like, "in your opinion, how does a person get to Heaven?" Now, he will say things like, "Well, none of us can really be sure. You just do the best you can." Is that what your definition is? No. We have different definitions. "Well, you must read your Bible and go to church." Is that how you go to Heaven? No. But, that is how he plans to go. I need to know what he is thinking.

The person will react the same, or most often will just agree with whatever you say.

(1) *Wait For Answers.*

Thinking takes time, give them time. Always remember that thinking is how we come to sort out all the facts, words, terms, and illustrations given to us. Remember, you have been around these spiritual words and terms for many years, but the child has not. The child has only been on earth six or seven years, that is it. Every big word he is not fully conscious of takes time to process. Oh, you know what you are saying, but you are not talking to yourself.

You must fight the tendency of allowing only four or five seconds to go by before you are ready to jump in with the answer. Silence is not a bad thing; it could actually be the best thing you do.

Obviously, you must "feel" when it is time to wait no longer. That time comes when you feel the child does not understand. Define, illustrate, or apply again and go back to the question again. Your goal is always for the child to express his own understanding in his own words.

My preference in leading children to pray is to give them a *"sample"* of what most people say to God when they want to be saved. We often call this the "sinner's prayer." For some children, they have never prayed to God before. And they certainly have not prayed to be saved. A sample prayer just gets in their mind what they will ask God for. But then I personally prefer the child to form that type of prayer in his own words, not necessarily "my words." You may have to, on occasions, break into his prayer to help him, as he forgets what to say to God.

(2) *Use non-judgmental responses to the child's answer.*

Negative responses to a child's answers tend to silence additional answers. You can always say "OK," "Fine," "All right," "Good," then follow it up by saying "Now, let's go over it again." This

Negative responses to a child's answers tends to silence additional answers.

allows you to correct the child, without being in the form of a put-down. This will not discourage the child, but will also lead you into clarifying anything still within question.

The excellent features about questions is that it keeps students listening, keeps them thinking, keeps their mind engaged with the topic, and it encourages them to keep talking to you.

(3) *The eyes will tell you so much.*

When communicating to a child, it is not just a matter of **what** we say, but **how** we say it. Eye contact is a must. Talk to the child, not to the Bible. Eye contact says, "I care," "I am interested in you." Call the child by name. This helps to personalize your comments. Do not be afraid to use a little humor. A smile goes a long way in opening the channels of communication, and helping a child relax around an adult.

Your eye contact to the child will also tell you if he is listening or not. His own facial expressions will often tell you he just did not get it. You need to be watching for the very same expressions you give off when bored stiff, or when confusion fills your mind. Get in front of a mirror and practice some of the obvious expressions that cover your face when you: question a thought, or you are thoroughly confused, or disinterested, or bored, or the eyes when you do understand. This reminds you again that you can also spot these expressions on "little faces" too.

I will never-ever forget the morning, in my own church, when a personal worker was on his knees at the pew talking to a bus child about being saved. Without even asking the child WHY he had come forward, he proceeded through the Romans Road. The problem is, the counselor never looked at the child as he read through the entire set of verses. He never asked the child if he understood, never illustrated, never got the child involved. The counselor did not know, although the entire church knew, that the little bus child was on the pew, turned around on his knees, waving to all the other bus kids in the back of the auditorium. At that time, all the bus children were in the main auditorium. I had to go over to the personal worker, tap him on the shoulder, and show him that the child did not have a clue that someone was talking to him. The point is, look at the child, talk to the child, and involve the child!

6. In The Middle Of Going- Walk Carefully

I have been in children and youth work for forty years, with twenty of those years at a church having over 10,000 in weekly attendance. The many experiences with children continue to remind me of two words: *Aggressive / Careful.* I want to be aggressively after children, because the "world" certainly is, but I also want to be very careful with these young minds.

Please understand that even though we talk a lot about being aggressive for Christ after children, we will also emphasize even more the word CAREFUL.

The opinions among church workers on the "age of accountability" are varied and probably always will be.

Children, even some into their late two's, can memorize the words they hear at church and quote them when called upon. But we would probably all agree the child does not understand what he is taking about. But, what if he is 4 or 5 or in 1st or 2nd grade? Is he now old enough? Is he now at the age of accountability? Is he now on his way to hell? He can say the exact words you said when God saved you, but does that mean he is saved? If so, let us give the next 200 kids we meet on the street a Snickers bar if they will repeat after us the sinner's prayer. Is it a set of spiritual words that makes everything right before me and my Lord?

The "age of accountability" does not come with chapter and verse. We would agree it is a good term to use in describing when it is time for a child to choose or reject Christ. But the problem comes with other "baggage," such as: Do they understand that their sin separates them from God and could forever separate them from Heaven? (There is that word <u>understand</u> again.) Do they fully understand that repentance from their sin and their unbelief is what stands between them and a saving (salvation) from their sin? Do they understand what God did for them and that He alone has the power and the willingness to forgive them of sin and to make them acceptable to God?

These are some big questions for little people. Yes, but is not that what must happen when one comes to Christ? Or, is there a simpler "child's way" and more complicated "adult's way"? Can a very young child understand what "lost" really means? Can one be saved until he sees himself lost?

Add to this the child's personal understanding level. Can a child be saved and not understand what it is all about?

Even though we do not find the "age of accountability" mentioned in Scripture, we still must consider both the *age* of the child and the *accountability* that he must face before his Creator God. His experience will be unique to him, and not based on

Are some children ready before others, even at the same age?

what a friend said, or did, or thought, or felt.

Is the child to the age of understanding that he is asking for Jesus Christ to rule and reign in his life! I am not talking about making Christ Lord of his life as a prerequisite to getting saved. But, would the child understand that this commitment is asking Christ to be hisLord and Master forever?

Are some children ready before others, even at the same age? Sure. Let us compare two children side by side. (1) In this chair is a child who comes from one of the finest Christian homes you could imagine. He has rarely, if ever, missed a Sunday school class. He has been in a Bible Club from three years old. He has gone to a Christian school from K-4. He has already memorized one hundred Bible verses. (2) In chair number two is a child that comes from one of the most ungodly homes in town. He has none of the above going for him. None. He has never heard the name of God other than by a cursing father. He can barely read, much less memorize verses. The Holy Spirit would be a "ghost" to him.

Are these two children different as to their readiness to come to Christ? Absolutely. Could they both pray the sinner's prayer tonight? Sure can. Would they both understand what they are doing? Perhaps neither, but we would certainly pick chair number one if we had to guess.

With some children, we are "pushing" too fast and too soon for them to say the sinner's prayer. What about their ability to grasp the abstract? They have never seen God or Christ. How can He hear me all the way from Heaven? How do I know if He hears me? How can I be sure my prayer worked? How does He come into me? Does it hurt? How big is He anyway? If we ever stopped long enough to ask a child if he understood, these are questions that are on the "inside" of a child's mind. Do you think every child you meet on the street is ready to be saved in 5-minutes or less? If they still believe in Santa Claus or the Easter Bunny or the Tooth Fairy, is he ready to believe in Christ?

Is the pressure we are exerting allowing the Spirit of God the timing that is His alone, not mine?

I am trying to impress upon you the **carefulness** we must always have in dealing with the children. If you are not willing to be in children's ministry for the long haul (putting time into little lives), then move on to the ministry of pew-sitting, and allow others to invest their life into these little lives!

That is why, in this book, we will mention the word UNDERSTAND so often. If the child does not understand, nothing real is going to happen. Whether it is Pastor's child or the head Deacon's child, *if he is not ready, he is not ready.*

Avoid the 5-minute dilemma we seem to have. Every child does not have to be saved in 5-minutes or less. With most children you will ever deal with, it takes time to deal carefully. Aggressive, yes! Careful, yes!

> *Every child does not have to be saved in 5-minutes or less.*

So, what we ask you to do is to consider the whole book. Yes, the "going" is still God's command, and all children have a right to go to Heaven, and the fields are extremely white right now, but we still want to do a full ministry with the children we reach.

Now, let us turn our attention on the potential of a child. They are some of the best years ever!

7. What Confuses Children?

May God help us not to be confusing to children. As you read over these thoughts, evaluate yourself, or some of your workers. Recognize that some change may be justified in your presentation to children.

1. Fast Talkers

We often forget that children have not been around as long as we have. They have not had long exposure to words and phrases and spiritual terms as we have. They cannot think and grasp understanding as fast as we can talk.

The younger the child, the slower we should talk. We do not talk "baby-talk," but we simply slow it down. It helps in two ways: (1) When I talk slower than normal, it constantly reminds me that I am talking to children. "Watch it, slow down, watch the words you say, watch the terms you use. Be careful."

As in teaching, I must always remember that I am not talking to myself, but to a child.

The second way talking slower helps is (2) it allows the children to stay with us easier. They have more time to "process" words and terms. That is why it is good for those dealing with children to "practice" sharing Christ with kids. Think through the best words and terms to use with different age groups. What are the best ways to illustrate sin, helping the children to grasp it better?

Think through the best words and terms to use.

Slow down, you are talking to children!

2. Words And Terms They Do Not Understand

Again, adults often assume too much. Just because a child nods his head in agreement, does not mean he understands what you are saying.

I understand, but does he understand? Take time, when you have settled on the best passage or group of verses for an age level, to look at the words in those verses.

Train yourself to stop and say, "I will need to explain and perhaps illustrate that word."

The words italicized below should run up a red flag in your mind, saying "stop and explain."

"As it is written, There is none *righteous*, no, not one:" Romans 3:10
"For all have *sinned*, and *come short* of the *glory of God*." Romans 3:23
"But God *commendeth* his love toward us, in that, while we were yet *sinners*, Christ died for us." Romans 5:8
"Wherefore, as by *one man* sin entered into the *world*, and *death by sin*; and so death passed *upon all men*, for that *all have sinned*." Romans 5:12
"For God so loved the world, that he gave his only *begotten* Son, that whosoever *believeth* in him should not *perish*, but have *everlasting life*." John 3:16

Do you get the picture? Just because you know what words mean like *believe, receive, condemned, death, everlasting, perish, come short,* or *the glory of God* does not mean the child does too.

Our problem is that often we never find out if they understand or not. We "rattle off" the Roman's Road or John 3 verses as if there is a set time we must beat. We ask few questions, therefore we often do not understand if he understands. We assume the child knows just about all that we know. That is called the "sin of assuming." Do not commit this sin.

3. A Non-Logical Presentation

Plans or ideas or concepts given without a logical step-by-step order are often very confusing. Again, you know what you are saying, but you are not talking to yourself. If their young mind cannot place the bits and pieces into a logical sequence, ending like a finished puzzle, then confusion probably still reigns.

The heart does not get excited about the end result unless the mind has sorted out the pieces and there is understanding present.

That is why planning and thinking- though *how* we share Christ is important. Although there are often variations we make in our presentation, having a sequence of steps in mind usually helps most people.

In our children's Club program, called Master Club, we have a merit badge for giving your testimony. Since other people will be hearing your testimony, why not give it in a way that others could know how to be saved too!

So, we teach our children how to give a testimony. Say more than "I got saved." Who saved you? Why did you need to be saved? Exactly what did you do to be saved? Bring the sequence out so someone else could also know how. Would someone else know how to be saved after you finished? Think it through!

At all costs, avoid confusion, slow down in your talk, think about the words and terms, asking always would the child understand? Then, at the end, ask them to tell you if they "got it" or not. In his own words, tell it back to you.

4. Too Much Explanation

Remember, we are talking to children. There needs to be that good balance of understanding and avoiding the confusion of too much explanation. That is why it is wise to do your homework.

We should picture giving the plan of salvation, and then think it through from their perspective. Think from the eyes of a child. Is it just too much? In a Gospel Tract, we try to do just that. The question is, **"Has it Happened Yet?"** Has what happened? The whole sequence revolves around the question, "Has there been a time when you received Christ as Savior?" This same question is asked about four times, because that is precisely the question of all questions we want to arrive to at the end of our presentation.

The tract then proceeds to answer how that receiving Christ takes place. Once they understand how to receive Him, then we are back to the original question, "Children, Has it Happened Yet?" If not, it could right now!

Simple, understandable, and logical are words we must remember.

Too much explanation confuses. We talk too much most of the time. Simple, understandable, and logical are words we must remember.

5. Counselors Assume Some Kids "Must Be Saved"

We all have to fight the temptation to assume that since our kids have been to Sunday school for ten years, without missing hardly a day, they "must" be saved. Sometimes, we may assume a child is saved because of "whose" child he is. I have seen preachers' children come to Christ who were quite mixed up. Deacons' kids, who were assumed to be saved years ago, finally get it settled.

Yes, a child can be saved at an early age of four or five. Over time, we have experienced many who, in their teenage years, just cannot remember it at all. Peace in one's own heart comes from knowing for sure that they know Christ, not from assuming they do.

Our role is to help the child sort it all out, to the best of our ability. And, as stated before, if the child is a church-parent child, work closely with the family.

I have met many former Temple students who come up to me and remind me that I was the one who dealt with them about salvation. This was after all their growing up years in a Christian home, a good Sunday school and church, and a Christian school. Now they are coming to a Christian college and are still not sure if they know Christ.

If your church has never trained people in dealing carefully with children, suggest that it would happen soon. Most churches have never helped the parents or even their own teachers. It is a must, for both!

Conclusion

Thank you for even picking up this book on **TEACHING!** Unfortunately, a multitude of teachers have never gone that far. They only teach the way one of their former teachers taught them.

I trust these thoughts will lead you to re-read again, to mark what you see that would improve your abilities and effectiveness in the classroom.

Could I encourage you also to be a life-long learner and a life-long reader. Never settle for less than a continuing perfection toward teaching.

Pray more than ever by name and by need for your students.

I believe that teaching God's Word is the largest role a lay person can do to serve the dear Lord. It comes with a price. That price is whatever is takes for you to be at your absolute best and always desiring to go farther. It always takes more to go farther for the dear Lord.

The dedicated teacher understands what that price is for them, and is found busy paying that price!

Could I refresh your mind once more on the most motivational thought I know that pushes teachers to be at their best every week:

"Your students are never more than one prayer away from making everything right with God."

And, it could happen in your classroom, before you say class dismissed. Therefore, I can't wait for my next time to teach!

Sincerely, Abb Thomes